Stanhopes of Elvaston

KAREN PROUDLER

First Published in Great Britain in 2016

By KP Publishing
Forge Cottage, Field Farm, Aston Lane,
Shardlow, Derbys DE72 2GX

Copyright © 2016 Karen Proudler

ISBN: 978-1-911472-03-2

Titles - Three Earldoms

CHESTERFIELD	**STANHOPE**	**HARRINGTON**
Created 1628	*Created 1718*	*Created 1742*
Extinct 1967	*Extinct 1967*	*current*

1st Baronet Stanhope of Harrington created 1605 for John Stanhope 1539-1620. At the extinction of the Earldoms of Chesterfield and Stanhope, their remaining and lesser titles passed to Harrington.

Current Earl of Harrington therefore has the following titles:
9th Viscount Stanhope of Mahon, from Letters Patent 2nd July, 1717
9th Baron Stanhope of Elvaston (Derby), from Letters Patent 2nd July 1717
12th Baron Harrington (Northants), from Letters Patent 6th January 1730
12th Viscount Petersham, from Letters Patent 9th February 1742

Arms:
Quarterly, ermine and gules

Crest:
Issuant from battlements of a tower azure, a demi-lion rampant or holding between the paws a grenade fired proper
Supporters:
Dexter: a talbot guardant argent gutte-de-poix
Sinister: a wolf erminois, each supporter gorged with a chaplet of oak proper
Motto: a deo et rege (From God and the King)

iv

Abbreviations

CKS   Centre for Kentish Studies
DRO   Derbyshire Record Office
LRO   Lichfield Record Office
UNMSC   University of Nottingham, Manuscripts & Special Collections

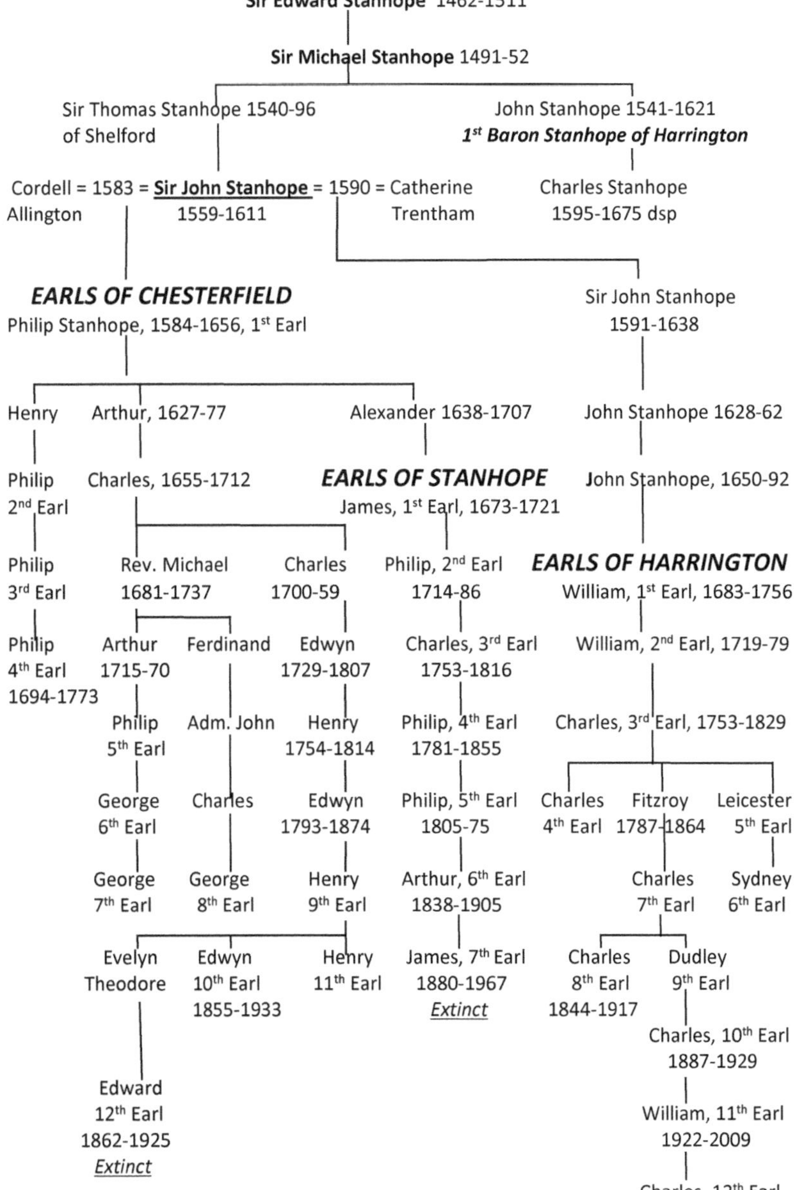

Sir Edward Stanhope 1462-1511
Sir Michael Stanhope 1491-52
Sir Thomas Stanhope 1540-96
of Shelford
John Stanhope 1541-1621
1st Baron Stanhope of Harrington
Cordell = 1583 = Sir John Stanhope = 1590 = Catherine
Allington   1559-1611   Trentham
Charles Stanhope
1595-1675 dsp
EARLS OF CHESTERFIELD
Philip Stanhope, 1584-1656, 1st Earl
Sir John Stanhope
1591-1638
Henry   Arthur, 1627-77   Alexander 1638-1707   John Stanhope 1628-62
Philip   Charles, 1655-1712   EARLS OF STANHOPE   John Stanhope, 1650-92
2nd Earl   James, 1st Earl, 1673-1721
Philip   Rev. Michael   Charles   Philip, 2nd Earl   EARLS OF HARRINGTON
3rd Earl   1681-1737   1700-59   1714-86   William, 1st Earl, 1683-1756
Philip   Arthur   Ferdinand   Edwyn   Charles, 3rd Earl   William, 2nd Earl, 1719-79
4th Earl 1715-70   1729-1807 1753-1816
1694-1773
          Philip   Adm. John   Henry   Philip, 4th Earl   Charles, 3rd Earl, 1753-1829
          5th Earl   1754-1814 1781-1855
          George   Charles   Edwyn   Philip, 5th Earl   Charles   Fitzroy   Leicester
          6th Earl   1793-1874 1805-75   4th Earl   1787-1864 5th Earl
          George   George   Henry   Arthur, 6th Earl   Charles   Sydney
          7th Earl 8th Earl   9th Earl   1838-1905   7th Earl   6th Earl
Evelyn   Edwyn   Henry   James, 7th Earl   Charles   Dudley
Theodore 10th Earl   11th Earl 1880-1967   8th Earl   9th Earl
          1855-1933   Extinct   1844-1917
                                                               Charles, 10th Earl
                                                               1887-1929
Edward   William, 11th Earl
12th Earl   1922-2009
1862-1925
Extinct   Charles, 12th Earl

Contents

Introduction

This book is a compilation of notes assembled on members of the Stanhope family who were connected with the family's estate at Elvaston in South Derbyshire. It is the result of the curiosity of a 12 year old, who cycled along the back lane from Alvaston to Elvaston Castle, newly opened to the public in 1970, and wondered about the former inhabitants. Though it has taken many years to be attempted, the result has finally satisfied that latent curiosity.

The Stanhopes were as varied as people in general are, and not all of them demonstrated reverence for their worthy ancestors. Philip Dormer Stanhope 4th Earl of Chesterfield, for instance, disposed of ancestral portraits by giving them away to his steward or throwing them out with the rubbish. Horace Walpole, writing in 1750, told how Philip mocked his lineage when he 'placed among the portraits of his ancestors two old heads inscribed Adam de Stanhope and Eve de Stanhope'. He was, however, the exception rather than the rule.

To counterbalance Philip's cavalier approach to his forebears, another Stanhope became a respected antiquarian; Viscount Mahon went to great pains to research and preserve as much detail as he could on the family's proud name and history. In 1855 he wrote 'Notices of the Stanhopes as Esquires and Knights, and Until Their First Peerages in 1605 and 1616'; an unpublished work which gave an excellent account of the earliest Stanhopes.

By way of introducing the Stanhopes, it is perhaps worth a few pages of print first to look at the family's origins and what manner of people they were.

Acquisition of Elvaston

The Stanhope family have been associated with Elvaston Castle and the wider estate for over 400 years and can trace their roots to the place-name 'Stanhope' in Durham from the 12th Century where early individuals of that place adopted the surname. Various antiquarians, such as William Camden and William Hutchinson concur[1] and, even the Stanhope family's own antiquarian Viscount Mahon, agree on their origins.[2]

These early Stanhopes were men of consequence in north-east England who held land and property granted to them by the king, in gratitude for their service to the Crown. One of the earliest, Sir Richard Stanhope c1260-1338, was also given a knighthood, most likely in respect

---

[1]   William Hutchinson, writing in 1794 'The History and Antiquities of the County Palatine of Durham', Vol. III, p352-3 said he believed the origin of the Stanhope surname 'to be denominated from a place of their own name (without doubt) the town of Stanhope, near a forest so called, in Darlington wapentake, in the bishopric of Durham.' Other sources too concur: A Dictionary of English Surnames by Reaney & Wilson, Oxford University Press, 1997 for one and also 'A Dictionary of County Durham Place-Names, 2002, p118 by Victor Watts

[2]   'Notices of the Stanhopes as Esquires and Knights, and Until Their First Peerages in 1605 and 1616', produced in 1855 by Philip Henry Stanhope, 5th Earl

of helping the king subdue the Scots when Edward I tried to impose his rule on Scotland. The reason for linking their 'rewards' and the king's gratitude for their service is to do with the fact that another Richard (son of above) received a grant of land and property in Hidegate, Berwick-upon-Tweed, an area that had changed hands repeatedly between England and Scotland through the years. In later years Richard moved south further into England where the antiquarian Collins recorded him as being called 'Lord of Elstwyke' - which is the old spelling for Elswick near Newcastle. Richard may have been a wool merchant but he also became Mayor of Newcastle and married a wealthy heiress.

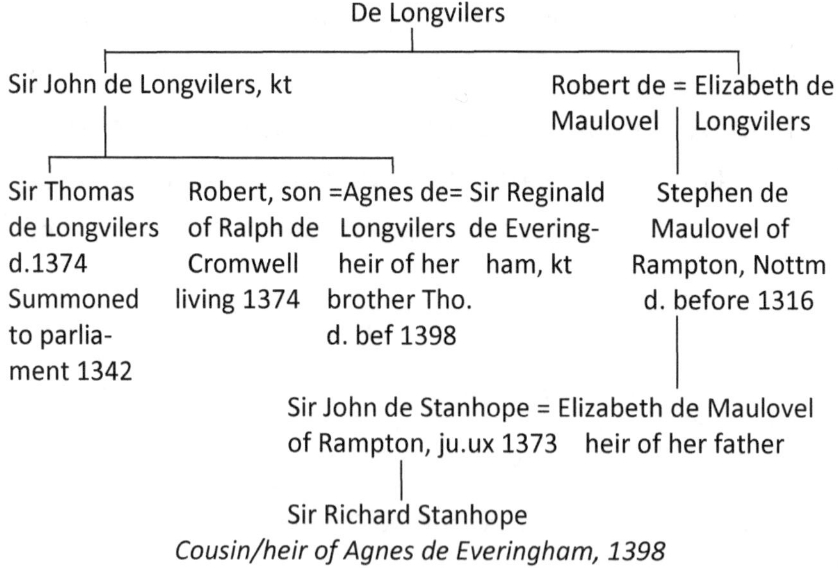

Richard's son John was, in many ways, the one who made perhaps the best match of all and also brought the Stanhope family to Nottingham. He was an elected burgess for Newcastle upon Tyne, served in Parliament, was elected Mayor, but more important than all of that was his marriage to Elizabeth Maulovel. This marriage brought inheritances not just from the Maulovel family, who owned the manor of Rampton in Nottingham but also the Longvilers of Tuxford in Nottingham.

With so many interests in Nottingham, John made the move south and settled his family in Rampton, north Nottingham. Of the importance of this family to Stanhope fortunes, William Camden wrote in 1586: "Shelford, where Ralph Hanselin founded a Priorie, and the Lords Bardolph had a mansion but now the seat of the worshipfull stocke of the Stanhopes, knights, whose state in this tract hath growne great and their name renowned since they matched with an heire of Mallovell".[1]

Richard, son of the above John Stanhope, was no shrinking violet. In 1411 there occurred a dispute between two families in Nottinghamshire. Alexander Meering (whose arbitrators were Sir John Zouch, Sir

---

[1]   William Camden, Britain, or a Chronological Description of the most flourishing Kingdomes, England, Scotland and Ireland 1586 - section on Nottinghamshire, Derby and Warwick

John Leek and Hugh Willoughby) was in a territorial dispute over Little Markham with John Tuxford (whose arbitrators were Sir Thomas Chaworth, Sir Richard Stanhope and Henry Pierrepont).

Stanhope had inherited an interest in this land and, after lengthy arbitration, the dispute remained unresolved. Sir Richard Stanhope began what his neighbours called, 'systematic intimidation' which left them in fear of their lives and, as a result of his behaviour, Stanhope was removed from the county bench in 1407. Hostilities continued through to 1411 when, for almost causing a riot, Stanhope and the other so-called arbitrators were imprisoned in the Tower of London on 24th October 1411. Although he was subsequently released and pardoned, he was further detained at Kenilworth Castle following the Leicester Parliament of April 1414.[1] The bitter enmity between these families seems to have continued through the generations as there were later disputes between the Zouch families and Stanhopes.

There followed a long succession of Stanhopes who were of high status, some being city burgesses, some being knighted or MPs and most, if not all, made fortunate marriages, often to heiresses.

---

[1]   Henry IV by Chris Given-Wilson, 2016

Michael Stanhope, son of Sir Edward was born into this Rampton family and, being the second son, was not expected to become his father's principal heir. His eldest brother married and had a daughter who, in time married and with that marriage a large portion of the Stanhope family's north Nottingham assets passed into her husband's hands. Fortunately, by the time this happened, Michael had found his own way of achieving advancement and expanded the family's fortunes in his own right. Most important to Michael's prospects, and the sealing of his eventual fate, was the fact that his father had married twice and Michael had a half-sister called Anne who, in the fullness of time, would marry Edward Seymour, later Lord Protector of England during the minority of Edward VI.

With the help of his family's good connections Michael secured a position in the noble household of Thomas Manners of Belvoir Castle, 1st Earl of Rutland, who was a favourite of Henry VIII. Through his mother, Michael could claim family connections with several of the leading families in Nottinghamshire; his mother Adelina was the daughter of Sir Gervase Clifton of Clifton and, through her, he was also related to the Pierreponts.

Michael had begun to get himself noticed when he demonstrated his loyalty to the Crown by helping to put down a rising in Lincolnshire headed by a farmer called

Kett. At the same time other developments paved the way for his advancement to a high position at court, when his half-sister Anne made an important match with Edward Seymour. The Stanhope family's connection with the Seymours coincided with King Henry VIII's marriage plans.

The king's faltering marriage to Anne Boleyn and the subsequent deaths of both his first wife Catherine of Aragon and the execution of Boleyn, left the king free to remarry, which he did with indecent haste. Just twenty-four hours after Anne Boleyn's execution, the king became engaged to Jane Seymour, sister of Edward Seymour mentioned above, and ten days later they married. The large extended Seymour family were now part of the royal family and Edward in particular immediately began receiving favours and honours from the king.

The tidal wave of gifts rippled out to Stanhope who, likewise, basked in the king's favour. He was appointed Esquire of the Body to the King and other appointments followed. His personal circumstances also improved dramatically and he was, like many others, well placed to take advantage of the king's dissolution of the monasteries when much land and property was freed up.

In 1538, by Letters Patent from Henry VIII, Michael

received the manor of Shelford and numerous other manors and rectories in Nottingham and elsewhere.[1] The following year, 1539, Michael acquired the tithes and ecclesiastical property of St Bartholomew's Church at Elvaston - a church founded by Ralph Hanselyn,[2] thereby beginning the Stanhope family's 400+ year association with that village. Many more manors and lands were acquired by him and, by 1540, Records of Enrolments show Michael and his wife Anne having widespread possessions across the three counties of Lincoln, Derby (Elvaston and Ockbrook) and Nottinghamshire.

Michael Stanhope's life, from this point on, was inextricably linked to his brother-in-law Seymour who, after the death of Henry VIII, became guardian to the young boy King Edward VI and he was made Lord Protector at this time. Seymour was the most powerful man in England and, as his brother-in-law, Stanhope rose to a powerful position on his coat-tail. He became the King's Groom of the Stool and had honours and good fortune heaped on him, enabling him to purchase some twenty manors for his family's prosperity.

---

[1]   Thoroton's History of Nottinghamshire: republished with large additions by John Throsby, Vol. 1. 1790

[2]   Shelford: an Augustine Priory, founded in the time of Henry II, by Ralph Henselyn, rents £151-14s-1d, now worth £3,034-1s-8d; granted 31 Henry VIII [1540] to Michael Stanhope

An estate at Elvaston was acquired by Michael before 1540, along with another 20 or so manors. It seems unlikely however that he had much opportunity to enjoy these acquisitions or spend much time, if any, in them as his presence was required at Court at all times though he kept a family residence at Beddington in Surrey close to the royal residences. Two years before Henry VIII's death, Michael was knighted on Trinity Sunday at Hampton Court following the king's return from Boulogne.

The death of Henry VIII led to a scramble for power. Amongst those charged with guardianship of Henry's successor, young King Edward VI, there was jealousy, intriguing and overt vying for power. Even Edward Seymour's own brother, in fact 'especially' from his brother Thomas Seymour, there was intense rivalry. Thomas begrudged his brother's exalted position and the fact that Stanhope had been placed so close to the king was further cause for jealousy by Thomas who felt that position should be his.

Unfortunately Thomas did not know when to quit. His ambition knew no bounds and his actions and behaviour eventually led to the council calling for him to be tried for treason. He was found guilty and executed by means of an order his own brother was required to sign.

This step had the effect of weakening Edward

Seymour's position as Lord Protector, as perhaps was intended by those in the council who wanted change. Charges, which were probably baseless, were then brought against Edward himself. The charge of treason was not satisfactorily proven but a lesser charge of felony was. The punishment, however, was the same whatever the charge was called and Edward was executed. Michael Stanhope, purely by his close association with Seymour, was dealt with in a like manner and was also executed.

Consolidation

The fact that the Stanhope family thrived so well after Michael's execution was largely down to his widow Anne, née Rawson, and her first-class family connections.

Cecil connections:-

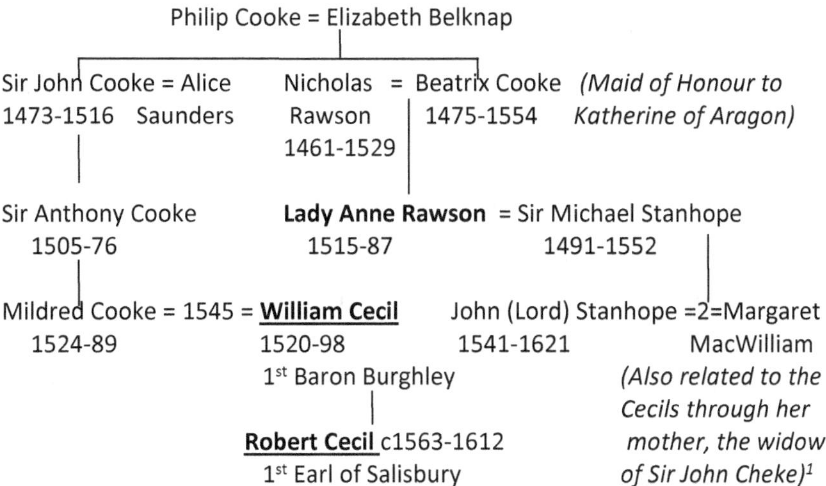

Through her mother, Beatrix Cooke, Anne was closely connected to some of the most influential people in the country, particularly Cecil, close adviser to Queen

---

[1]   In 'The Elizabethan World' by Susan Doran and Norman Jones, 2014, it is said that she was Mary Hill, daughter of Henry VIII's Sergeant-of-the-Cellar Richard Hill. That she had married in 1547-8 Sir John Cheke (humanist and Greek scholar) and then married Henry MacWilliam who subsequently became Gentleman Pensioner. She was called Lady Cheke. William Cecil's first wife was Mary Cheke, sister of John Cheke

Elizabeth. Anne would repeatedly make use of Cecil's goodwill to her family and, by his patronage, her sons were brought into parliament and the court.[1] This continued the Stanhope family's restoration which had begun when the Catholic Queen Mary had reigned and she had restored many of their lands and manors to them.

Visiting Elvaston

Whilst it is doubtful that Michael personally visited Elvaston, it is known for certain that his eldest son and heir Thomas did. It took many years, following his father's execution in 1552, for Thomas to acquire parts of his father's estate; some had been sequestered, some were restored by Queen Mary and he needed to wait for the land to be surveyed until about 1577.

Around this time Thomas had set up a meeting at Elvaston to visit and evaluate the estate with Lawrence Wright, his agent who had formerly worked for John Port, Thomas Stanhope's late father-in-law.[2] Stanhope was accompanied by Sir Thomas Manners (uncle of the

---

[1] There was also a relationship between the Stanhopes and Hoby family, through the marriage of Elizabeth Cooke to Sir Thomas Hoby, brother of Sir Philip, Master General of Ordnance and English Ambassador to the Holy Roman Empire

[2] TNA: STAC 5/S82/12 South v Stanhope, Fenton & others. Answer of Sir Thomas Stanhope and TNA: STAC 5/S29/15 Stanhope v Russell & others, Complaint of Sir Thomas Stanhope

Earl of Rutland and brother-in-law to the Earl of Shrewsbury) and they were accompanied by a group of servants; a total party of around 17 persons.

They arrived at Elvaston where Stanhope may have been trying to get Manners to lease the hall itself or some part of the estate,[1] but his efforts were in vain as the condition of the hall/estate was considered poor and the offer was not accepted. Stanhope's party retired for the evening to accommodation in the centre of Derby at the Talbot Inn in Irongate, near to Derby Cathedral, that being the main inn in town.[2]

This visit to Elvaston and Derby was memorable for the fact that Sir John Zouche heard of Stanhope's visit and, being his enemy,[3] Zouche gathered a force of armed supporters and they made their way to Derby Market Place baying for blood and an encounter with Stanhope. Zouche and his supporters stayed at an Inn on the nearby Cockpit Hill and the whole town was

---

[1]   HPT, Hasler, Ed., Vol. 3, pp9-10, accessed 30th July 2014; TNA: STAC 5/S3/17 Souche [Zouche] v Manners, Scryvyn, Revell, Kingston, Hill. Answer of Sir Thomas Manners and TNA: STAC 7/29/48 Sir Thomas Stanhope v Sir John Zouche, deposition of Lawrence Wright

[2]   The Talbot Inn was on the west side of Irongate, the same side of the street near the corner of Sadler Gate

[3]   Thomas Stanhope had been accused by Sir John Zouche of making defamatory comments about Zouche's wife in 1577. There was also a dispute between the families over property belonging to Sir John Zouche which had been sold to Thomas Stanhope by Zouche's son William. Calendars to the Proceedings in Chancery in the Reign of Queen Elizabeth, Vol. 3 from the Originals in the Tower, 1832

awash with rumours of an impending confrontation. Appeals were made for calm and the town bailiffs rang the church bells to alert the townsfolk to rally in support of maintaining the peace. In the end there was no riot and peace was preserved though the incident was followed up at the assizes in Derby and, for the most part, Zouche was held to be the aggravating party.

The incident is recorded in the annals of Derby history as follows: "1576: In this year a great number of persons assembled by Sir John Zouche and Sir Thomas Stanhope, should have fought, but were restrained by the burgesses and ringing the town's bell."[1]

It is probably fair to say, however, that Stanhope who 'may' have been the aggrieved party in this particular instance, could be every bit as provocative and intimidating as Zouch.[2] He frequently quarrelled with neighbours and his name was often cited in Privy Council meetings for offences such as theft, slander and, even, defacing a parish church.[3]

The land at Elvaston had been rented out by the Stanhopes for quite a few years prior to this and, in the meantime, Thomas had been busy expanding his

---

[1]   A Collection of Fragments Illustrative of the History and Antiquities of Derby by Robert Simpson, Vol. 1, 1826
[2]   Early spellings for Zouch are Zouche; and for Port are Porte
[3]   Acts of the Privy Council APC, x pp165-6, p412 and p172

holdings in the area. The funds for these acquisitions were from his wealthy heiress wife, Margaret Port, who after his death complained *"I brought to my husband … a thousand marks by year of good land, his estate then being so mean, that though he gave me all he had, yet [he] was not able to make me above £60 by year for my jointure. From which my lands being by him leased twice over, he raised such great fines, and with that money bought so many lordships and manors as I may truly term myself, not merely the foundation, but the builder up and establisher of his present house"*.[1]

She was right. Indeed in 1568 the extent of his land at Elvaston was: 20 messuages, 10 tofts, 2 water mills, duckhouse, 22 gardens, 300 acres of land, 30 acres meadow, 200 acres pasture, 250 acres gorse and furze, 26s rents, fishing in the Derwent, view of frankpledge [joint suretyship] in Elvaston, Thulston, Ambaston, Alvaston, Boulton, Ockbrook, Spondon and the rectory of Elvaston, for the sum of £100. Five years later, in 1573, he had 40 messuages, 40 tofts (homesteads), 6 dovecotes, 8 gardens, 8 orchards, 2,000 acres of land, 600 acres of meadow, 2,000 acres of pasture, 20 acres of wood, 2,000 acres of furze and heath, 40s rents in Elvaston, Ambaston, Thulston, Alvaston, Spondon,

---

[1]   Centre for Kentish Studies, Maidstone: U1590 C2/9. Discourse of Sir Thomas Stanhope 'regarding his wyves behaver sens the tyme of this my loung and grievous sickness' and reply by M Stanhope HMC ref 49/12

Boulton, Chellaston, Draycott and fishing rights in the River Derwent.[1]

In 1585, three years before she died, Dame Anne Stanhope (John's grandmother and widow of Sir Michael who was beheaded), signed over her life interest in numerous estates to her eldest son and heir Sir Thomas.[2] Since John had just married, it seemed to be an appropriate time for Thomas to settle parts of the estate on John, his eldest son and heir and this is most likely to have been the catalyst for John's settlement at Elvaston around this time.

---

[1]   DRO: D518/MF/2 Final Concord between Thomas Stanhope, Lawrence Wright and Edward Windsor, knight
[2]   DRO: D518/MF/7 Stanhope of Elvaston Papers, Earls of Harrington. Grant by Dame Anne, widow of Sir Michael Stanhope, dated 1585/86

Arrival of the Stanhopes

SIR JOHN STANHOPE (the Elder) 1559-1611 (n.s.)

After the death of Sir Thomas, his eldest son and heir John Stanhope took over, that is 'despite' rather than 'because' of his mother Margaret's endeavours. Margaret (née Port) had her own agenda and clearly begrudged her late husband's control over the huge dowry she brought to their marriage. After his death, she moved frantically to gain control of any and every aspect of the Stanhope estate she could for herself and her Port relations. She spent her final years being taken to court by her husband's executors, his siblings and even by her eldest son John and she refused to obey any and all instructions from the courts over administration of her husband's estate to the point that she ended up in the Fleet prison, several times.

In Stanhope family history, there can be few figures as pivotal as Sir John Stanhope. It was from him that the three earldoms of Chesterfield, Stanhope and Harrington descended and it was his decision to divide his estate between the eldest sons of his first and second marriages that shaped everything that followed.

Shelford/Elvaston

John was educated at home before attending Eton and Oxford where he received B.A. His relationship with his father, like that of his younger brother Edward, was strained as his father also considered him rebellious and John spent some time abroad. He attended Grays Inn, after which the good Cecil looked for a place at Court for him. His parents' plan for him to marry a Clifton heiress did not come to fruition as there was a change in the fortunes of the Clifton family and, as the eldest son and heir, it was essential for John to make a match which would enhance the family's fortunes.

As well as being the progenitor of all the Stanhope earldoms (Chesterfield 1628-1967; Stanhope 1718-1967 and Harrington 1742 to present), John seems to have been the first of the family who resided at Elvaston in Derbyshire. Though his grandfather Michael acquired the estate and his father Thomas widely expanded the family's holdings in that area, John left the family home at Shelford after marriage and settled himself at Elvaston.

At the age of about 24 in 1583, John married Cordell Allington,[1] third daughter and co-heiress of Richard Allington of Lincoln's Inn and Jane Cordell. Within a year

---

[1]   DRO: D518M/F5-6 and TNA: C142 280/90, Thomas Stanhope's Inquisition Post Mortem

Cordell had given birth to twins Philip and Thomas, though only Philip survived to adulthood. It is perhaps likely that Cordell died in childbirth as one year later, in 1585, she died after giving birth to Cordelia Stanhope. Although the Will of John's second wife refers to Cordelia as her daughter, the fact of her birth date being the same day that Cordell died and, indeed, the very fact she was named Cordelia, all suggest that Cordelia belonged to John's first wife, though she was of course brought up entirely by the second.

This arrangement is confirmed in an agreement dated 18th June 1607 when young Cordelia's marriage settlement was being set up and the document refers to Cordell's jointure and settlement on her heirs.[1] The parties involved were Sir Roger Aston (Cordelia's husband), Sir John Stanhope (her father), Sir Thomas Aston of Aston (her father-in-law) and others, including Lawrence Wright of Snelston, her father's trusted agent and friend. The document is endorsed 'My Lady Aston's Joynture of Cranford' suggesting that Cordelia, now Lady Aston, acquired the manor of Cranford for her jointure. Sir Roger Aston was a courtier and one of King James I's favourites (to whom he was Gentleman of the Bedchamber) though he was the illegitimate son of Thomas Aston the Sheriff of Chester in 1551. Roger's

---

[1] London Metropolitan Archives: City of London ACC/0530/ED/01/009 dated 18th June 1607

first wife had been of the blood royal, being Mary, daughter of Andrew Stewart, Master of Ochiltree. Cordelia and Roger had one son who died young. By this marriage Cordelia became sister-in-law to John Knox, a prominent leader of the Protestant Reformation.

Precisely which structure John and Cordell resided in at Elvaston from 1588 is not clear. See date 1633 below.

Since the oldest surviving part of the present day Elvaston Castle has 1633 inscribed in a lintel (see above) on the south facing wall, then John must have lived in an earlier hall, perhaps the one his father surveyed and found decayed. It would be John's son, also called John (the younger) and who died in 1638, who had the hall rebuilt in his lifetime.

The following list shows periods of ownership of Elvaston Hall or Castle by Stanhopes, though is not a precise catalogue of periods of residence because, for example, Charles Stanhope may have acquired Elvaston and the estate at his father's death in 1730 but he would have also resided there as a child etc. So it is a list of ownership rather than actual residence, which may have been longer:-

Date Range:	Tenure:	Owner/Occupier:
1539		Sir Michael Stanhope of Shelford - acquired land & advowson of Elvaston
1573		Sir Thomas Stanhope of Shelford - visited, enlarged land holdings
1585		Lady Anne Stanhope signed over further lands to Thomas (including some at Elvaston)
1588-1610	**22 years**	**Sir John Stanhope (the elder)**
1610-1638	**28 years**	**Sir John Stanhope (the younger)**
1638-1662	24 years	John Stanhope
1662-1692	30 years	John Stanhope
1692-1730	38 years	Thomas Stanhope, oldest brother 1st Earl
1730-1760	30 years	Charles Stanhope, older brother 1st Earl
1760-1779	19 years	2nd Earl, William Stanhope
1779-1829	50 years	3rd Earl, Charles Stanhope
1829-1851	22 years	4th Earl, Charles Stanhope
1851-1862	11 years	5th Earl, Leicester Stanhope
1862-1866	4 years	6th Earl, Sydney Stanhope
1866-1881	15 years	7th Earl, Charles Wyndham Stanhope
1881-1917	36 years	8th Earl, Charles Augustus Stanhope
1917-1928	11 years	9th Earl, Dudley Stanhope
1928-1929	1 year	10th Earl, Charles Stanhope
1929-1930s		11th Earl, William Stanhope
		Left Elvaston for Limerick, Ireland

Date Range:	*Tenure:*	*Owner/Occupier:*
1939-1950	11 years	Teacher-Training College during WWII years
1963		Death duties forced sale to Needlers Dev. Co.
1963		House contents sold at Sothebys Auction House
1964		Further house contents sold at estate
1969		Castle and 130 hectares estate bought by Derbyshire County Council and Derby Corporation
1970		Estate opened to the public as a Country Park
2009		Estate surveyed to establish £6m repairs needed
2013		Derbyshire County Council consider the estate's Future
2014		Public consultation on Castle and Estate's future
2016		Proposal to appoint a Trust to manage estate

One of the earliest documents which links John Stanhope with Elvaston is a conveyance dated 28th June 1588 which states "conveyance of above property by Richard Wendesley of Melbourne, John Brickerton of Derby to John Stanhope of Elvaston".[1]   So clearly John was established at Elvaston well before his father's death in 1596, after which event his uncles were on hand to render him assistance in managing his affairs and the estate.[2]

John's first wife Cordell died a year or two after their marriage and, within a short space of time, he was looking for another bride. When Catherine Trentham appeared in John's life as a potential second wife for

---

[1]   DRO: D518M/T91 and D518M/F8, 9, 10 Conveyance to John Stanhope

[2]   DRO: D518M/F8-9 Consent to trustee and Edward, 2nd son of Sir Thomas Stanhope deceased to alteration of uses under indenture 17th Feb 1583/4 of messuage and lands in Derbyshire and Staffordshire, which also includes a conveyance by John Stanhope of other lands in Burton Joyce, Nottingham to the same use

him, his parents made it known that they did not approve of the match as Catherine was not a woman of good fortune, her father being in debt to the Stanhopes. On 12th January 1597/8 he assigned his interests in the manors of Elvaston, Ambaston, Thulston, Toton and lands in Alvaston, Boulton and Barton-in-the-Beanes to his wife Catherine for her jointure.[1]

As previously mentioned, John's father Thomas had been on poor terms with most of his neighbours in Derbyshire and Nottinghamshire and, in particular, he had clashed with Gilbert Talbot. This Talbot-Stanhope feud was extended to include John when Sir Charles Cavendish (son of Bess of Hardwick who was married to Gilbert's father) challenged John to a duel.[2] This episode, however, slipped into farce when, after much protraction and deferment, at long last a time was set for the duel to take place, only for it to be discovered that Stanhope was wearing an unusually thick doublet; the purpose of which, it was claimed, was merely for protection against the cold. John subsequently spent a few days in jail for disobeying the Queen's instructions not to get involved with Cavendish.

---

[1]　DRO: D518M/F10 Deed of assignment from John Stanhope to wife Katherine

[2]　Sir John Stanhope had accused Zouche of embezzlement of funds which had been raised in 1569 to suppress the Rebellion of the North. Calendar of the Manuscripts of the Marquis of Bath: Talbot, Dudley and Devereux Papers 1533-1659

Dissatisfied Talbot supporters subsequently resorted to scouring Cheapside in London to find Stanhope and, on receiving promising intelligence on his whereabouts, went to Fleet Street to the Three Tons Tavern and lay in wait for their quarry. When Stanhope appeared, the Talbot supporters attacked him. This incident was followed by a retaliatory assault in Kirkby, Northamptonshire when Stanhope had Sir Charles dealt the same treatment. You might say the Stanhopes were the ultimate victors as John, 4th Earl of Clare (Stanhope descendant) married Margaret, daughter of Henry Cavendish and, as there were no children from this union, the Cavendish inheritance passed to the Stanhopes.

John Stanhope's difficulties with his mother Margaret continued meanwhile and, faced with her absolute refusal to hand over essential documentation, he had removed them from her house whilst she had been incarcerated in Fleet prison for not complying with court orders. With the help of his uncles, who were executors of his father's Will, John managed to get, for example, rectory and glebe lands at Spondon away from his mother's control. He did this by purchasing the lease (in Lawrence Wright's name) and, when the rents were unpaid, was able to acquire the estate. His uncles were interested parties as Thomas's Will had made bequests to them and so they looked on John to settle up, since

Margaret was being uncooperative.

Just before John was knighted in 1603, he co-signed an indenture with his uncles on 29th October 1602[1] when, together with trustees, lands were assigned over to John, with remainder to his uncles.[2]

His mother's recalcitrance caused John financial hardship, as she held much of John's inheritance as her jointure. This resulted in John having to borrow (according to him) £2,000 for his maintenance. His mother, meanwhile, was yet again taken to Fleet Prison for non-compliance with court orders and failure to hand over rents.

With further help from his uncles, John managed to arrange his affairs. His eldest son from his first marriage, Philip, married in 1605 to Catherine Hastings, grand-daughter of Dorothy Port (Philip's grandmother's sister). This marriage, therefore, probably pleased his mother Margaret (née Port) and John drew up a 100 year lease around 1607 of the bulk of his estates due to Philip on his death. However, he held back a substantial number of manors, including Elvaston, Ambaston, Thulston, Boulton, Alvaston and Osmaston which he

---

[1] DRO: D518M/F11 Indenture between John Stanhope of Elvaston and his uncles

[2] Staffordshire Record Office: D641/4/J/4/3/36, dated 31st Jan 1600. Sir John Stanhope acknowledges that he has received £30 from Edward Sulyard for a horse to go to Ireland (Sulyard was a recusant)

wished to give to his eldest son John from his second marriage. This was the time when the Stanhope family's vast estates became divided, instead of channeling everything through to Philip.

Philip received: the manors of Horsley, Horston, Woodhouse, Kilburn, Spondon, Stanley, Cubley, Marston Montgomery, Hilton, rectory of Horsley, Musden Grange in Staffordshire, manors of Stoke Bardolph, Shelford, Newton, Kneeton, Gedling, Carlton, Radcliffe-on-Trent, advowsons of Horsley and Radcliffe-on-Trent, Middleton or Old Barton Park, parishes of Longford and Barton, 'Little Haw Grange' messuage and parishes of Dale and Stanley.[1] Philip was also an heir to other large fortunes, including that of his grandfather Sir John Port and the Hastings, Earls of Huntingdon family too.

PARTIES:

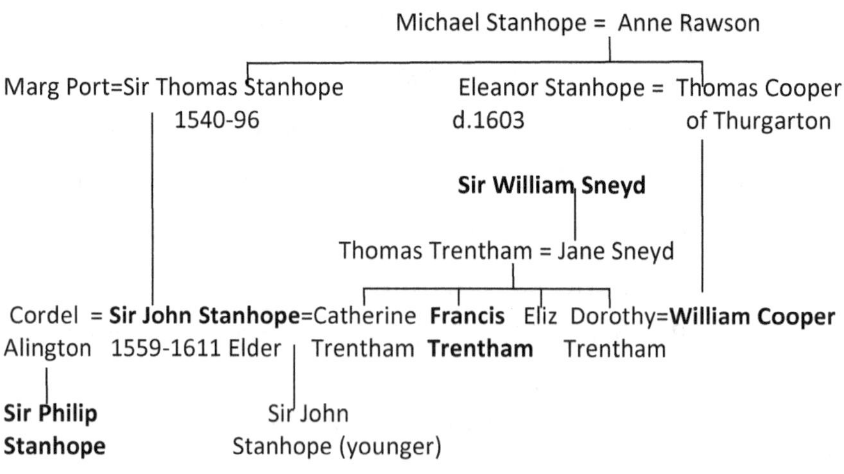

---

[1]   DRO: D518M/F55-6 dated 18th June 1607 Lease for 100 years to Philip Stanhope from his father John

The division of his estates was made in an Indenture of 18th June 1607 between various parties, shown above. It was a post-nuptial agreement which gave Catherine Trentham's children as good an inheritance as Philip Stanhope; hence the preponderance of Trentham relations as parties.[1]

John and his second wife Catherine Trentham had ten children, though some died young, and the last child was born after John's death, the child being called John Posthumous Stanhope. Catherine was the daughter of Thomas Trentham of Rocester in Staffordshire and her sister Elizabeth was the Countess of Oxford being married to Edward de Vere, 17th Earl of Oxford.

Another event occurred around this time which focused the family's attention on inheritance with the marriage of John's eldest son (from his second marriage) who married around 1608 to Olive Beresford. He had continued to expand the family's assets, however, such as on 21st June 1608, when he acquired land and messuages at Ockbrook from Frederick, Lord Windsor.[2]

This particular acquisition, however, was the subject of a chancery bill later when his aunt, Dorothy Port

---

[1]   DRO: D518M/F55-6, dated 18th June 1607 Lease for 100 years to Philip Stanhope from his father Sir John Stanhope (the Elder)
[2]   DRO:D518M/T257-9 Deed to Sir John Stanhope for £18 from Frederick, Lord Windsor of the manor of Ockbrook

(Hastings, Countess of Huntingdon) brought proceedings against John over some aspect of Ockbrook Grange (late the possession of Sir John Port).[1]

It would appear from the litigation that followed Sir Thomas Stanhope's death, that his widow Margaret (née Port) disposed of the family's assets in a way that her husband's siblings did not approve of. Sir Thomas Stanhope's home at East Stoke, for example, was sold to George, Earl of Huntingdon, Margaret's brother-in-law and this sale was disputed later in chancery when Sir Edward Stanhope (brother to Sir Thomas) brought legal action against Margaret (and Sir John Hollis) over the sale.[2] Indeed, a glance at the chancery records during John's lifetime and the multiple cases he was involved in seems justification for families, such as the Stanhopes, sending their sons to the Inns of Court and entering Parliament as a necessary means to equip their heirs with the legal skills and political influence to defend their estates and interests.

Each time a key heir in the Stanhope family died,

---

[1]   TNA: C2/Jas1/H13/15, Countess of Huntingdon [Dorothy Hastings, née Port] v Sir John Stanhope & Richard Coxe, 1603-25

[2]   TNA: C78/133/22 dated 2nd May 1604 Stanhope v Stanhope (Edward Stanhope v Margaret Lady Stanhope, Sir John Hollis and John France). Sir Edward (2nd son of Thomas) had been involved in litigation against Margaret, but the date of this action being 1604 (when Sir Edward died in 1603) perhaps suggests it was his younger brother who took over the litigation, he was after all a Doctor of Law

there was a raft of litigation between family members, such as when Sir Thomas died. There was also litigation after John himself and his wife Catherine died because it appeared that John had sought to prefer his second family over his eldest son Philip who was already very well provided for. Then, when wife Catherine died, her Will gave preference to her daughter and son-in-law John Holles. No surprise then that there was subsequent litigation between Sir Philip Stanhope and Sir John Holles.[1]

When John came to write his Will in July 1610, he made mention of the fact that he had already provided for his two eldest sons; Philip had received a substantial legacy from his grandfather's Will of the manors of Bretby and Sawley and a host of smaller manors in addition to a sizeable inheritance from John Molineux.[2] John made mention of his debts "which are not small" and he took pains to ensure that daughters and young children were provided for as well as wife Dame Catherine.

Lawrence Wright, whose name features in many documents connected with Stanhope, was singled out and described as "my most true friend" and he was

---

[1]   TNA: C2/Jas1/S2/5 Stanhope v Holles (Sir Philip Stanhope v Sir John Holles)
[2]   DRO: D518M/F54 Lease for 600 years by Sir Philip Stanhope of Bretby to trustees of the manors of Bretby and Sawley

tasked with ensuring John's unmarried daughters received the proceeds of the sale of lands at Weston which John had been inherited form his uncle Edward.[1]

A few months after he wrote his Will, there appears on record for 29th December 1610, a further settlement for wife Catherine involving her brother Francis Trentham of Rocester, Staffordshire. In the covenant, John made over additional property to Dame Catherine and their children, that is to say Humberholme in Osmaston, lands which he had recently purchased from Richard Dale. In addition he made over to his second wife and children from their union, all lands and property he had inherited from his uncle Sir Edward Stanhope (Doctor of Law).[2]

It is to be wondered how fit John was at the moment of this settlement being created because within a few short weeks, there was a further covenant on the same

---

[1]   DRO: D779B/T 176 is an Assignment showing that it was William Stanhope (brother of Sir John Stanhope the younger) who, as Executor of his mother Dame Catherine, was instrumental in bringing about the lease of the lands at Weston which had been bequeathed by Sir Edward (Letters Patent 20 July 1594 from Queen Elizabeth) to his nephew Sir John who, in turn devised the lands to his daughters Catherine, Dorothy and Jane. They gave them in trust to their mother and William, in accordance with their mother's Will, leased the lands for the benefit of the daughters. Selling to John Gage of Firle in Sussex and Thomas Stich of London. The extensive lands covered Weston, Aston and smaller sections in Shardlow and Wilne. See also DRO: D3155/6761 Grant William Stanhope, Katherine, Dorothy and Jane Stanhope to John Gage and Thomas Stick dated 22nd June 1621

[2]   DRO: D779B/T 20 Post-Nuptial Settlement John Stanhope/Cath. Trentham

issue: between Richard Dale of Osmaston and the now widowed Dame Katherine Stanhope, widow of Sir John, decd, regarding Humberholme. This agreement is dated 12th March 1610/1611 and so clearly Sir John Stanhope died between 29th December 1610 and the following March 1610 (o.s.) 1611 (n.s.)[1] with the Will proved in May 1611. His mother Margaret managed to outlive him by two years.

When wife Catherine wrote her Will nine years later, she desired to be buried "neare unto my late good husband in the vault wh'ch I made in the chancel at Elvaston". She left land and money to her youngest son John Posthumous and other sons too. There is an interesting reference to her building expenses "I do require and charge my said son Sir John Stanhope, as well in part of performance of his father's letters written unto him, and in respect of the great charge I have been at in building for him". It is not clear which building structure Catherine was referring to since the oldest part of Elvaston Castle carries the date 1633, so perhaps she commenced the building of that structure and her son completed it, or the building work may refer to Shelford or another of the family's possessions. In the Church at Elvaston there is an effigy of Sir John Stanhope in armour alongside his wife.

---

[1]   DRO: D3155/6618 Covenant, Richard Dale of Osmaston and the widowed Dame Katherine Stanhope of Elvaston, widow of Sir John, dec'd

Catherine (Trentham) and husband Sir John Stanhope
Alabaster effigies

JOHN STANHOPE (the Younger) 1591-1638

Eldest son and heir John Stanhope of Elvaston was about 19 years of age when his father died but had already been knighted by King James I at Whitehall and was married shortly after. On 21st May 1607 the marriage settlement was agreed between John Stanhope and Olive Beresford,[1] daughter of Edward Beresford of Beresford, Staffordshire[2] concerning manors of Elvaston (including advowson of church), Thulston, Ambaston, Borrowash, Toton, Barton-in-the-Beans and the advowson of Spondon church. Additional lands included Morley Park in Duffield and Belper, Bayliff Close, Spondon, Southhouse Grange in Stanley Dale, and lands in Borrowash. Trustees were to be Richard Cope and Robert Purefoy and the manors were to be settled on the heirs male of John and Olive. [3]

---

[1]   DRO D518M/T281 Limitation of Uses, Sir John Stanhope ref daughter Olive, 29th October 1620

[2]   DRO: D664M/F1 Marriage Settlement, 1607

[3]   John's name appears in an Indenture dated 1619 where his brother-in-law Thomas Cockayne (married to sister Anne Stanhope) conveyed the manors of Ashbourne, Great Clifton and Little Clifton, which he had inherited from his father Sir Edward Cockayne 1551-1606 dec'd, to John's half-brother Sir Philip Stanhope for 60 years at £44 per annum. Northampton Record Office: C3199 Indenture Agreement to Convey from Thomas Cockayne to Philip Stanhope with the approval of Sir John Stanhope of Elvaston, dated 20th March 1619

Section of Elvaston Castle on the south side (corner of east building) which dates back to 1633.[1]

---

[1]   Picture taken 26th May 2016, after removal of scaffolding for roof repairs to the east of the building

Civil War Years

Some account of the Stanhopes at Elvaston at the time of the Civil War was recorded by a close relation, Lucy Hutchinson. Lucy's husband John was the step-son of Lady Catherine, sister of Sir John Stanhope,[1] relationships show below:

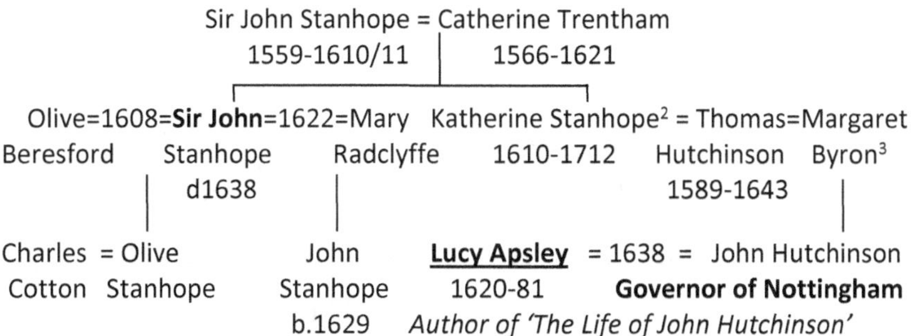

Her husband was Governor of Nottingham and became

---

[1]   Memoirs of the Life of Colonel Hutchinson, published by J Hutchinson: To Which is Prefixed The Life of Mrs Hutchinson, written by herself. Edition 2, Longman, Hurst, Rees, Orme, 1808

[2]   Nottingham Archives: M/704, accession no. 7245 dated 20th December 1671. These Hutchinsons were of Owthorpe in Nottingham viz: Deed of trust 1) Dame Katherine (Stanhope) and C [Charles, her son] Hutchinson, 2) Sir Francis Butler (first wife was Isabella Butler) and A [Alexander] Stanhope (Alexander being a son of Sir John Stanhope), 3) F Tudor and J Jeffs to hold Owthorpe Manor for a yearly rent of £200

[3]   Margaret Byron was of Newstead Abbey and would be related to the later celebrated Lord Byron. There was a further connection with the Byrons in that Mary Radcliffe (wife of Sir John Stanhope) was the grand-daughter of John Radcliffe of Ordsall and Alice Byron

one of the regicides when called on to sign Charles I's death warrant. Being so closely related to the Stanhopes it is likely Lucy's account is somewhat biased in their favour but it is interesting nonetheless.

SIR JOHN GELL

In the years before the Civil War there had been hostility between the Stanhopes and Sir John Gell,[1] now the Sheriff of Derby who, in 1635 had been charged with raising £3,500 from the county for the unpopular Ship Money.[2] Lucy described what happened when Gell challenged Stanhope:

> *"Sir John Stanhope was sent for up by a sergeant-at-arms, his misdemeanour thus: the Sheriff demanded of him what he was assessed at for the shipping-money. He answered he had no money, but offered to show him plate or cattle: the sheriff took some cows to raise the money and drove them away, not putting them off suddenly he sold them under the money Stanhope was set at, so comes again to drive more. Sir John Stanhope, a*

---

[1]   Sir John Gell 1593-1671 of Hopton Hall, Derbyshire
[2]   DRO: D258/23/20/16 Letter from John Gell to Edward Nicholas regarding Sir John Stanhope of Elvaston and problems of collecting ship money, dated 1635

choleric man, withstands the sheriff's bailiffs, gives them ill words, and he and his men rescue the cattle from them. He is not yet come to answer this: the sergeant returned with affidavits from the neighbour justices, that he is so afflicted with the stone and pains of the gout, that he cannot stir without danger of his life".[1]

Stanhope was in poor health from 1635 onwards, as he was suffering from cholera, stones and gout. That is perhaps why it was his wife's name[2] which appears on a draft petition in 1635 to Parliament complaining about John Gell's distraint of their property in respect of ship money.[3] Wife Mary and brother Philip, Earl of Chesterfield, combined to take their complaint on John's behalf about Gell to the Privy Council but received no sympathy from them.

Gell was unable to get the better of Stanhope, who died in 1638, and was probably wary of making such a

---

[1]   Cited in Life of John Hutchinson of Owthorpe, p352 but taken from Stafford Correspondence, Vol i, p505, 8th January 1635/6 Mr Garrard's letter to Stafford. The account is confirmed by records in the Calendar of Domestic State Papers for 1635 and 1636

[2]   DRO: D258/56/6 Mary Stanhope's description of Gell harrying her husband for Ship Money

[3]   DRO: D258/30/6 Draft Petition of Dame Mary Stanhope to Parliament against John Gell's distraint

powerful local man an enemy. With the arrival of Civil War and Stanhope's death, however, he seised an opportune moment to take revenge on other Stanhope family members.

In his Will, John had left a modest sum of £5 to his half-brother Philip, Earl of Chesterfield, 20s to sister Lady Okehampton (Cordelia Stanhope), 20s to brother William, 20s to sister Anne Cockayne, 20s to sister Lady Huchinson (Kathleen Stanhope), 20s to sister Sutton (Dorothy Stanhope), 20s to sister Lady Mountnorise (Jane Stanhope) and £20 to brother John Posthumous Stanhope. Then, in a codicil dated 9th June 1638[1] he left larger sums of £1,400 to daughter Elizabeth, £1,000 to son Cromwell[2] and £500 to daughter Anne. Byron was to have £250 plus land.

It is curious that the main Will did not include the children yet the codicil written the same day did. That may, however, have been because it concerned money given to the children by Dame Alice Radcliffe, their grandmother. A second codicil dated 20th March mainly

---

[1]   DRO: D518/MF/16 Probate of Will of 12th March 1638 for Sir John Stanhope of Elvaston

[2]   The choice to name one of their sons Cromwell was connected to the family's association with Thomas, Lord Cromwell 1594-1653 - cousin of the Parliamentarian Oliver Cromwell. Thomas was a Royalist in the Civil War. Sir John Stanhope co-signed a grant when Thomas Lord Cromwell acquired the Barony of Lecale in Ireland (LRO: S.MS.360/5/1 dated 12th September 1633). Thomas was later made 4th Lord Cromwell, 1st Earl of Ardglass

concerned an annuity to John's brother John Posthumous Stanhope and land he held called Humberholme. This second codicil mentioned the fact that the stables at Elvaston had yet to be completed (house dated 1633). Sir John said there was just a little more to do but that "his ladie would doe". He wanted to be buried in Elvaston Chancel with his parents.

John Stanhope 1591-1638. This is the effigy destroyed by Gell's men. It was reassembled in 1731 by his great-grandson Charles.

Right: Wall plaque in Latin, transcription below.

To the memory of John Stanhope died 1638

Here rests regretted by all and calmly awaiting the second coming of Christ His Redeemer John Stanhope, Knight, who, as not having sprung to no purpose from a most notable stock adorned with his personal virtues the nobility of his family, controlling all his impulses by the power of his intellect and for strength of mind most admirable. By his discharge of offices in the County of Derby with unshaken integrity he wisely sustained his honour, and rendered faithful service to his king as well as diligent service to his country having been elected to Parliament. The poor were defended by his patronage, fed with his hospitality and relieved by his munificence, while the best of the nobility delighted in his friendship and in the charm of his conversation. He died in the year of our Lord 1638 in the ..... year of his age. By his first wife, Olivia, the daughter and heiress of Edward Berrisford in the County of Stafford, he had only one daughter, who was married to Charles Cotton, Esquire and by his wife Mary, daughter of John Radcliffe of Catsal, in the County of Lancaster, knight, who survived him, he became the father of 7 sons and 3 daughters. Of these he lost in their infancy two sons and one daughter, John, Thomas and Frances, while John, Cromwell, Radcliffe, Byron, Alexander, Elizabeth and Anne still survive. This monument of her love was dedicated to her dear husband by the right noble lady, Mary, his disconsolate widow."

This monument of his ancestor having been reduced to fragments by the ravages of time, was restored by Charles Stanhope, Anno Domini 1731 (great grandson of Sir John Stanhope).

JOHN STANHOPE 1628-1662

Lucy Hutchinson's account of events at Elvaston during the Civil War continued ...

> *"The account given of his devastations at Elvaston is thus confirmed by 'Mercurius Aulicus' for Feb. 15, 1643. From Derbyshire the carriage and behaviour of Sir John Gell, the ringleader of the rebels there, was certified in these words that follow: - 'Sir John Gell with his forces consisting*

of about 400 men came to Elvaston in Derbyshire, an house of the Lady Stanhope's, widow of Sir John Stanhope's, to whom Gell (though never a friend), yet in his lifetime durst not declare himself an enemy. But after his death, making use of the power given him by the fundamental laws of the kingdom, he plundered his house of all the arms, money, and goods of worth he could find, to the value of £1,500. Not contented with this, and to make it more plainly appear that his coming was as much for malice as plunder, he went into the garden (in which the good lady, taking very much delight, had made it a very pleasant place, with handsome walks and diversities of the best flowers), which he caused to be digged up and utterly ruined. He left not here, but to add more to her vexation, and to please himself in doing mischief, he went into the church, where she had lately erected a tomb for her husband which cost her £500, that he caused to be demolished, and the stones to be broken into several pieces, that no possibility was left to repair it. But his act of greatest inhumanity was to go with his soldiers into the vault, where the dead of the family were usually buried, and to run their swords through their dead bodies".

Gell similarly plundered another Stanhope residence, being the Earl of Chesterfield's house at Bretby. The Civil War saw Chesterfield and Gell on opposing sides and, with Gell appointed Commander-in-Chief of Parliament's forces tasked with securing Derby, Chesterfield lost his son in the conflict and was subsequently imprisoned and died whilst still incarcerated.

How these circumstances changed so dramatically is impossible to tell, yet Gell (her husband's protagonist) did end up marrying the widowed Dame Mary Stanhope on 25th September 1648. His reasons for doing so, according to Mrs Hutchinson, were that he wished to discredit the Stanhope name, to destroy the glory of her late husband's house and good name. She wrote *"He (Sir John Gell) pursued his malice to Sir John Stanhope with such barbarism after his death that pretending to search for arms and plate, he came into the church, and defaced the monument that cost six hundred pounds, breaking off the nose and other parts of it; he digged up a garden of flowers, the only delight of his widow, upon the same pretence; and thus woo'd that widow who was, by all the world, believed to be the most affectionate and prudent of woman-kind; but, deluded by his hypocrises, consented to marry him, and found that was the utmost point to which he could carry his revenge, his future carriage making it apparent, that he sought her for nothing else but to destroy the glory of her husband and his house".*[1]

It is apparent, however, from the raft of litigation that followed their marriage, that Gell was not successful and so his comments were probably made after-the-fact and were an effort at face-saving.

A chancery bill of 1651 from Mary's sister-in-law Anne Stanhope was brought against Sir John Gell and Dame Mary Gell (nee Stanhope), his wife, over property of the Kniveton family from which it is clear that Gell's motives in marrying Mary were pecuniary. Some rough notes were compiled[2] which show Gell had anticipated (or had been told by Mary) that she had a large estate worth 10,000 including gold, money and jewels but, it seems, the shrewd Mary Stanhope had conveyed her estate

---

[1]   Memoirs of the Life of Colonel Hutchinson, p107 by his wife Mrs Hutchinson
[2]   DRO: D258/20/1/4 Rough Notes on the Bill of Complaint of Sir John Gell against Dame Mary Stanhope

some five or six days before marriage in trust to Sir John Curzon and Alexander Radcliffe. Sir Alexander Radcliffe[1] was Mary's brother and, it is said, he carried the purple robe at the coronation of Charles I; the other trustee for Mary's estate was Sir John Curzon whose daughter Jane was Dame Mary's daughter-in-law, but who was also closely related to the Gells.

Gell himself was in difficulties by this time as he had been implicated in a plot to restore Charles II. He was tried and found guilty of treason and sent to the Tower of London for life. His subsequent appeal for clemency was eventually successful and he was released in 1652 and pardoned the following year, by which time Dame Mary had extricated herself from association with him and, by her shrewd handling of her estate, avoided what could have been a wiping out of the Stanhope fortunes at Gell's hands.[2]

Further documentation, dated 1654, shows one of Mary's sons, Cromwell Stanhope, making a deposition on his mother's behalf in the same matter[3] as Gell had clear designs on Mary's jointure. By this time Mary had died and Gell was seeking administration of his late

---

[1]   Sir Alexander Radcliffe 1608-54 of Ordsall

[2]   TNA: C6/39/112 Gell v Stanhope, dated 1653. Also, DRO: D258/18/18/18 Note of bills and answers in Gell v Stanhope and D258/20/1/2 Further Answers of John Stanhope to the Bill of Complaint of Sir John Gell

[3]   DRO: D258/20/1/3 Answer of Cromwell Stanhope to the Bill of Complaint of Sir John Gell, 1654

wife's estate and going after the personal estate of Sir John Stanhope,[1] which was being resisted by the rest of the family. As Gell had handed over his Derbyshire estates to his son in 1646 and died with modest wealth, it seems unlikely he was successful in claims against the Stanhopes.

JOHN STANHOPE 1650-92

John, son of above, married Dorothy Agard, daughter and co-heir of Charles Agard of Foston. The Agards of Foston were Royalists in the Civil War and the family may have had part of their estates sequestered. Charles Agard was Sheriff of Derbyshire in 1661 and was appointed to a commission to seize the property of recusants in Staffordshire in 1674/75. The marriage settlement is dated 27th October 1677[2] and the marriage portion figure was £1,500 but Dorothy also shared with her siblings Katherine and Vere Agard in a moiety of the advowson of Mevesyn Ridware in Staffordshire[3] which she brought with her to the Stanhopes by marriage.

In the Will of Charles Agard of 22nd May 1680 the bulk of his estate was divided between his wife and son

---

[1]   TNA: C6/135/93 Gell v Stanhope. John Gell v John, Byron, Cromwell and Alexander Stanhope, also Thomas Ellys (Holles) and wife Anne (Stanhope) dated 1655

[2]   DRO: D664/M/F/3 Marriage settlement of John Stanhope of Elvaston and Dorothy Agard, dated 1677

[3]   DRO: D518M/F84 Moiety of advowson of Mavesyn Ridware, Staffordshire

equally. Agard left his son-in-law John Stanhope "his black stoned colt" and to his daughter Dorothy £10 to buy a piece of plate. Most of Charles Agard's manors, not affected by entail, had been sold in 1678/9 to Thomas Orme to settle debts and legacies to his sons and youngest daughters.[1]

THOMAS STANHOPE 1680-1743 - eldest brother of 1st Earl of Harrington

John Stanhope and Dorothy Agard had three sons, only one of whom had sons to continue the line.

Eldest son Thomas succeeded his father and was MP for Derby 1702-5 and, although he died without heirs, his marriage to Jane Thacker[2] (who was the widow of Charles Stanhope, son of Philip, Earl of Chesterfield) did have the effect of bringing together two separate branches of the Stanhope family. Jane was the daughter of Gilbert Thacker of Repton and his co-heir.

On 12th July 1718 when his cousin James Stanhope was advanced to Baron Stanhope of Elvaston and Viscount Stanhope of Mahon after a successful military and political career, Thomas was named as the default

---

[1]   DRO: D384/Z/Z/7 Probate of Charles Agard of Foston dated 22nd May 1680

[2]   These Thackers were descendants of Thomas Thacker who, in 1538, was granted the manor of Repton from Henry VIII, to whom he had been servant. Gilbert Thacker died in 1712 and the Repton estate when to his daughter as heir

name in case James should die without male heirs. He was further made Earl Stanhope in 1718, a title which continued to his sons right through to 1967 when the title became extinct on eventual failure of issue. When Thomas died childless in 1730 he divided his estate between his wife and brothers Charles and William. To brother William, 1st Earl of Harrington, he gave £3,000 plus all his land at Repton which had been acquired from his sister-in-law Mary Thacker.

CHARLES STANHOPE, brother of William 1st Earl of Harrington 1673-1760

After the death of Thomas without heirs, the next to succeed to the Stanhope estate at Elvaston (and beyond) was his brother Charles who did not marry. Charles outlived his younger brother William who became 1st Earl of Harrington, and so Charles named his nephew William (2nd Earl of Harrington) as his heir. Like his elder brother, Charles Stanhope entered Parliament in 1714, being Under Secretary of State to his influential cousin James, at the commencement of the Hanoverian era and became Secretary of the Treasury and Treasurer of the Chamber in George I's time.

Charles was just 12 years old when his father died and, after completing his legal training and being called to the bar, he was ready at the end of Queen Anne's reign to receive the benefit and patronage of his cousin,

James Stanhope, who had been appointed Secretary of State for the Southern Department. It was the start of the new Whig Georgian era and James secured a post for Charles as his Under-Secretary. A few years later, on Walpole's resignation from government, Charles moved to the Treasury as his cousin James took over as First Lord of the Treasury and Chancellor of the Exchequer.

Appointments and promotions at this time were heavily predicated on the system of patronage and, whilst Charles owed his advancement entirely to his cousin's influence, the sudden death of James in 1721 left him exposed. Not entirely friendless, but vulnerable without his patron.

Cousin James Stanhope had suffered a seizure whilst speaking in the House of Lords about the developing crisis of the South Sea 'Bubble' and, ironically, Charles was thought to be heavily involved in scandal surrounding the same issue where it was alleged that he had been accepting bribes. Records of the Sword Blade Company (brokers for the South Sea Company) showed Stanhope's name listed as someone in receipt of a bribe in return for his parliamentary support of the company; it was said that he had received a large portion of shares without any payment having been made. There seems to be plenty of evidence that Charles was deeply involved in the stock, acting as a conduit for family members to acquire shares. His involvement was investigated in a secret parliamentary commission in February 1721: There were two allegations against Charles:

1. That "10,000 South Sea stock was taken in for his benefit, by Robert Knight, without any valuable consideration; and that the difference arising by the advanced price thereof was paid him out of the cash of the South Sea Company";

2. That "Elias Turner & Co had bought 50,000 stock at a low price of the South Sea Company, in the name and for the benefit of Charles Stanhope, the difference of the advanced price whereof, amounting to 250,000 had been paid to the said Charles Stanhope by Sir George Caswell & Co."[1]

The second allegation concerned a huge sum of £250,000 which was shown in the company's records against Charles Stanhope's name, but subsequent enquiries suggested the possibility that this record had arisen without Stanhope's knowledge and so the issue was dropped. The first charge was examined by the parliamentary committee:

"Sir John Blunt being again examined, informed your committee, that Mr Knight had the chief management of

---

[1]   The South Sea Bubble by Lewis Melville, 1921. Pp220-221

the disposal of the Company's stock; and, that whilst the South Sea bill was depending in the House of Commons, Mr Knight acquainted him, that Mr Charles Stanhope, one of the secretaries of the treasury, desired to have 10,000 l. stock bought, or taken in, for him, at the market-price, which was then about 250l. per cent but the said Mr Stanhope did not absolutely agree to have the stock at that time; but the same day, or the day following, Mr Knight shewed Sir John Blunt a letter, signed Charles Stanhope, where he desired to have the said 10,000 l. stock bought, or taken in, for him, and Sir John Blunt consented that he should have it accordingly. That on the strictest enquiry your Committee cannot discover that the said Mr Stanhope ever paid, or gave any security to pay, for the said stock, or that any actual transfer was made to him of it. Mr Richard Holditch being again examined, said he understood by Mr Knight that 10 or 12,000l. of the Company's stock, said to be sold was held for Mr Charles Stanhope of the treasury. That Mr Knight told him, that the said Mr Stanhope was undetermined, in the morning when he first mentioned it, whether he would have it or no, but in the evening agreed to have it. Your Committee find upon inspection of the account of cash kept by the South Sea Company with the Bank of England, that by notes drawn upon the Bank by the cashier of the South Sea Company the sums following amounting to 51,736 l. 13s were paid to Charles Stanhope Esq one of the secretaries to the treasury, out of the cash of the South Sea Company, at the days following viz: May 7th 5,662l. 13s; May 12th 600l. June 18th 40,609l. September 10th 4,865l."[1]

---

[1]   Cobbett's Parliamentary History of England: 1714-22, Vol. 7 by Great Britain Parliament, William Cobbett, Thomas Curson Hansard, pp721-722

Stanhope, responding in the House of Commons, stated that he was innocent of any wrong-doing and gave a speech which included many references to his cousin James, 1st Earl Stanhope. It was said many of those listening could not bring themselves to vote against anyone connected with the respected Earl. So, by strenuous exertions of Stanhope relations and even involvement by the King, the secret committee was prevailed upon to acquit Stanhope though the subsequent motion and vote was lost by a narrow 3 votes only. However, the sense of "no smoke without fire" led to any future appointments for Stanhope being deferred. Any sign of favour in Stanhope's direction would have ignited animosity from those who felt sceptical at his acquittal.

In effect, Charles Stanhope, made £250,000 from the South Sea shares which, according to him, was done by the company's brokers and without his knowledge. Little wonder that many onlookers were somewhat mistrusting of his claims of innocence. Charles felt that the matter had ruined his career and said "this is the cruellest usage of me in the world, and is what must forever ruin my reputation and fortune"[1] and subsequently put the blame on Walpole.

---

[1]   Stanhope to Newcastle, 19th August 1721, BL Add. MS 32686 fols. 181r, 184r

After 1734, when he was returned as MP for Harwich, he voted against the government, though refrained from voting against the removal of Walpole at the end of his career. Charles held on to a position in government to 1727 but, upon George II ascending to the throne, the King blocked Stanhope's appointments after he found a note written by Charles, at the height of the dispute between George I and II, when Charles had suggested George II be kidnapped and put in exile.

As time went by he was frozen out of government posts and turned his attention to his domestic responsibilities. One of the purchases Charles made with his accumulation of cash was the Manor of Sawley, not too far from his Elvaston estate which he had purchased from his cousin the Earl of Chesterfield. He died on 16th March 1760 unmarried. He bequeathed this manor to his nephew the 2nd Earl of Harrington who he made his principal heir. Another major beneficiary of his Will was Philip 2nd Earl Stanhope, son of James of whom he said "as a mark of the love and esteem I ever had for the late James Earl Stanhope".

The Will of Charles Stanhope reflects the coming together of the Stanhope branches because, apart from him leaving his estate to his Harrington nephew, he also left bequests to relations on the Earl of Chesterfield's line too. Rev Michael Stanhope (grandfather of 5th Earl of Chesterfield) who wrote his Will in 1737, requested that Charles Stanhope assist in the advancement of his children and, although Charles did leave substantial legacies for two of Michael's children, Captain Thomas Stanhope and Lovell Stanhope who became Under Secretary of State in 1764-65, Lovell's advancement and later appointment to high office was due to his relation the Earl of Chesterfield rather than Charles. Bequests were also made to Philip 2nd Earl of Stanhope. Charles thus left substantial bequests to all the Stanhope lines of descent: Harrington, Stanhope and Chesterfield. Although administration of Charles' Will was granted to nephew William, 2nd Earl of Harrington, William never got around to executing the Will and it lay in abeyance.

Bachelor Charles resided, when in town, in St James Parish, Westminster and, although he had no children to provide for, his Will does mention one family in particular who were residing with him at Elvaston Castle/Hall - the Severns. Charles Severn was his Steward and had his brother and sister living at Elvaston, so too was a Mrs Catherine Severn and her two daughters.

Earls of Harrington

WILLIAM STANHOPE 1683-1756 -1st Earl of Harrington

Portrait by Sir Godfrey Kneller. Oil on canvas 73.5 x 60.3 cm.

Public domain

Diplomat and Whig Politician

William was the fourth (3rd surviving) son of John Stanhope and Dorothy Agard and, as such, was not expected to be troubled by being his father's heir. Indeed the death at a young age of one brother and the inheritance of his two elder brothers, Thomas and Charles, meant the family's inheritance by-passed him, though since both brothers died without male heirs, the titles and inheritances would later fall to his son who was also called William.

Like many younger sons, William looked to the army for his first career and, after attending Eton and the Inner Temple, he obtained a post as Lieutenant and Captain of the 2nd Foot Guards (Coldstream Guards). The War of the Spanish Succession, to prevent the French House of Bourbon taking the Spanish throne and becoming an overwhelming power in Europe, saw Stanhope serving in Spain and the Low Countries under Charles Churchill who, by 1707, became Colonel of the Guards with Churchill's older brother Marlborough being in overall command.

Stanhope rose rapidly through the ranks to become a regimental colonel towards the end of Queen Anne's reign. Following the 1710 general election, however, which saw a Tory victory, there was a marked drop in enthusiasm for continuation of the war and Marlborough was out of favour. The Queen had a falling out with the Duchess of Marlborough and some parliamentarians claimed that Marlborough and his cronies only wanted a continuation of the war to enrich themselves, which many had done through making use of their regimental allowances.

Stanhope stayed in the army long enough to secure a colonelcy but the death of Queen Anne in 1714 brought about a sea change in politics. The new House of Hanover favoured the Whig party and thus began an era of long domination of Whigs in Parliament. There was a scramble by all those wanting to be part of the new regime and, for his part, William Stanhope obtained a seat as MP for Derby. In both the army and his subsequent career in the government, William had the benefit of his cousin James, 1st Lord Stanhope, being prominently placed as Commander in Chief of the British Forces in Spain and then in September 1714, James was appointed Secretary of State for the Southern Department and became one of the Chief Ministers. Older brother Charles also entered parliament at this time as Under Secretary of State to cousin James too. William's oratory skills as a parliamentarian were perhaps questionable as, according to Horace Walpole, he was "without either the talent of speaking in Parliament, or any interest there".[1]

Stanhope MPs for Derby:-

Thomas Stanhope	1702-05	Older brother to 1st E Harrington
William Stanhope	1714-22 & 27	1st Earl of Harrington
Charles Stanhope	1730-36	Earl of Chesterfield line (cousins)

In the 1715 Jacobite Uprising, he once again donned his army cap and took part in the suppression of James Stuart's attempt to seize the throne but William's military activities were sporadic after this time as his diplomatic and parliamentary career took off.

Throughout William's time in politics, relations with

---

[1]   Horace Walpole: Hervey 1.4

Spain were to figure large as a fellow colonial power. The uneasy peace which followed the cessation of hostilities at George I's ascension required the presenting of compensation claims from British merchants to Spain and this task fell to William when, on 19th August 1717, he was appointed Envoy Extraordinary and Plenipotentiary to the King of Spain. Arriving in Madrid in October of that year, he wrote to Henry Worsley a few weeks later on 17th December and described the city as "so dead and barren a place as to all engagements".[1]

The following year William was sent to Italy where, from 17th November 1718 he was Envoy and Plenipotentiary to the Court of Turin. His cousin James Stanhope's principal objective at this time was to prevent an Austro-Spanish war over territories in Italy and so William's appointment was key to tackle the most important foreign policy issue of the moment. Making use of his experience at Madrid where Spain's Cardinal Alberoni was known to be a hawk set on war, Stanhope had a difficult time with diplomacy. On 20th June 1718 he received a letter from Admiral Byng indicating the King of Spain had designs on Italy and the hopes for a diplomatic solution seemed dashed. Writing to Worsley again, on 9th September 1718, Stanhope

---

[1]   BL: Add. MS 15936, p146v

warned that talks were not going well and war was probably inevitable.[1] It was shuttle diplomacy and, after Stanhope had been refused an audience with the King of Spain, he was next sent to France.

At this time William married Anne Griffith in March 1719 (younger daughter of Lady Mohun and her first husband Edward Griffith), by which marriage the Stanhopes acquired an estate at Gawsworth in Cheshire (which had been inherited from the Gerards - once Earls of Macclesfield). Stanhope later purchased Gawsworth and Bosley manors in 1727 from the trustees of his wife's marriage settlement. Within a year of being married, Anne died in childbirth after giving birth to twin sons William (heir) and Thomas.

On 31st May 1719 William returned to military service via Paris and was a volunteer in the French army under the Duke of Berwick's camp at Fontarabia where he spent the summer. It was reported that he headed up an English squadron which attacked a prize ship at St Anthony in the Bay of Biscay and destroyed the naval stores contained in it. His courageous spirit was recorded thus: "finding it necessary to encourage and animate troops which had not been use to enterprises by sea, he was the first that leaped into the water when the boats approached the shore".[2] He was consequently

---

[1]   BL: Add. MS 15936 pp 166-167

promoted to Brigadier-General.

William returned to England in December when his wife gave birth to their two sons and she sadly died after childbirth. Six months later, through the patronage of Lord Townshend, Stanhope obtained an appointment as British Ambassador Extraordinary and Plenipotentiary in Madrid with the difficult task of containing Spain's demand for Gibraltar to be returned to it and its continuing desire to encroach on Italy. William's difficult diplomatic mission received the full backing of the King who dogmatically refused the surrender of Gibraltar and gave William his whole-hearted support. William was in the fortunate position of being supported by his own King and was now well thought of by the King of Spain who said of him "Stanhope is the only foreign minister who never deceived me".[1]

In 1723 Stanhope had some health problems and requested a return to England for a while. This return would, he hoped, allow him some time to gauge his standing with the current administration. He explained in a letter to Sir Luke Schaub: "to know thereby the true foot upon which I stand with the Ministers, in order to take my measures thereupon for continuing much

---

[2]   The Gazette, no. 5773

[1]   History of England: from the peace of Utrecht to the Peace of Versailles, 1713-83, Vol 1 p363

longer here or not".[1] The result of his sojourn was that William felt sufficiently empowered to return to Madrid as Ambassador and continue his diplomacy which, at times, gave him great frustrations. The necessity to tell the Spanish court that it was not possible to return Gibraltar to them led to William writing to Townshend in 1725 complaining about "the almost utter improbability of avoiding a speedy rupture with Spain".[2]

During his time in Madrid, William witnessed many historic events which he made mention of in his dispatches, such as the abdication of Philip V, succession of Louis, return of the Spanish Infanta, the separation of Spain from France and union with the House of Austria.

In 1726 one of Stanhope's colleagues at the Spanish court, Ripperda who was one time Prime Minister of Spain, got into difficulties after he had been accused of misappropriating large sums of money and was dismissed from post. Ripperda considered Stanhope a close friend and so sought refuge with Stanhope in the British Embassy. Stanhope's opinion of Ripperda, however, was far more measured and he gave little credence to his opinions and had, in any event, left the embassy for a visit to Aranjuez the previous day. *"On*

---

[1]   BL: Add. MS 4204, p113r, William Stanhope letter to Sir Luke Schaub, dated 22nd March 1724 n.s.

[2]   BL: Stowe MS 256, p34r William Stanhope letter to Lord Townshend

returning home that evening, Mr Stanhope was not a little surprised to find in his apartments the lately arrogant Prime Minister of Spain imploring his protection. Nay, more, so unmanned was Ripperda by his misfortune, and so grateful when Stanhope consented to shelter him, that he proceeded to disclose the highest secrets of his state. He communicated the particulars of the private agreement at Vienna, declaring that it aimed at nothing less than a total extirpation of the Protestant Religion; and that the King of Spain had said, that for such an object he would willingly sell his very shirt".[1] All his testimony was apparently presented with *"the greatest agonies, and frequent burst into tears"*. After several days of Stanhope refusing to give up his charge, the authorities intervened and took Ripperda by force from Stanhope's protection and the former Prime Minister was taken into custody as a prisoner at the Castle of Segovia where he was incarcerated for two years on charges of treason.

William Stanhope's 'Memorial to the King of Spain', 13th July 1726 n.s.

> *"Sir, The underwritten Embassador Extraordinary and Plenipotentiary of his Britannick Majesty, having received Order to communicate to your Majesty the Sentiments of the King his Master, upon the Duke of Ripperda's taking Refuge in his House at Madrid, and his being taken from*

---

[1]   Mr Keene's Memoir for the Duke of Newcastle, 15th June 1726

thence by Force by Virtue of your Majesty's Orders: And having at the same time received the Copy of a Letter which the Duke of Newcastle, Minister and Secretary of State, was ordered to write to M. De Pozobueno, your Majesty's Minister at London, exhibiting amply the King's Sentiments on this Affair: The said Embassador judges he cannot better acquit himself of this Duty, than by delivering to your Majesty the annexed Copy of the said Letter, as containing literally all that he has been commanded to represent upon the said Transaction; without adding any Thing of his own, more than most humbly to beseech your Majesty to be pleased to have Regard to the solid and just Reasons therein alledged; promising himself, from your Majesty's high Wisdom and Justice, all necessary Reparation of the Violence, done to the Immunities of publick Ministers; and to have the Resolution communicated to him which your Majesty shall judge proper to take in this important Case; that he may be able to give an Account of it to the King his Master. Done at Madrid the 13th of July, 1726. Wm. Stanhope"[1]

Stanhope was wary of the King of Spain's wrath when news of Ripperda's presence in his house became known, so insisted that the King be informed and, in turn, received an assurance from the King in person (having had an audience with him on the 16th) that no fault lay in Stanhope's person, though the King was unhappy that Ripperda had sought refuge in a foreign minister's home.[2]

The King of Spain was nervous about any disclosures

---

1   Historical Register No. XLV by C.H. Green, p22
2   Historical Register No. XLV by C.H. Green, p25

Ripperda might make to Stanhope and Stanhope's letter, above, was an attempt to ameliorate those concerns. Whatever Stanhope committed in writing was not the full extent of Ripperda's testimony which he thought too dangerous to commit on paper including as it did the Spanish court's intention to invade England, so instead sent Mr Keene to brief the Duke of Newcastle, who in turn would brief the King, on what information had been gleaned, of which detail the Treaty of Vienna was of paramount interest.

Having thus been careful to keep good relations with the King of Spain, Stanhope was very unhappy when the King sent 60 soldiers to forcibly remove Ripperda as he considered that this action was an infraction of the Law of Nations. Ripperda was taken away and incarcerated in Alcazar in Segovia.

In respect of Stanhope's general performance as ambassador, it was said he was remarkably well informed of events around him, having *"spies in all parts of the court and in all the public offices, so that he got immediate information of the most minute particular. The friars who had access to the most considerable houses by their employment of saying masses for the dead, were all in his pay"*.[1] He was described as a

---

[1] Lives of Cardinal Alberoni, and the Duke of Ripperda, Ministers of Philip V ... by George Moore

patient and calm man who would never interrupt those who spoke to him and the contrast between him and Ripperda who disclosed his testimony in floods of tears, is stark.

The information he had extracted from Ripperda, or rather that Ripperda had been so keen to divulge, changed opinions in London and Britain subsequently despatched a naval fleet to the Spanish coast which caused alarm in Madrid. Stanhope's diplomacy with Spain was becoming harder and harder to maintain as an undeclared war between the countries developed. Stanhope stayed in post as long as he could and, when he did leave Madrid which, of necessity had to be done without taking leave, his contribution was widely applauded, in particular by the King. Writing to Stanhope, Newcastle concurred with this good opinion and said *"had it been possible for all the prudence and Attention that Man could employ, to have prevented their [Spain] running so wild and extravagant a way of acting, you would have succeeded in it"*.[1]

From 1725 to 1730 William was the colonel of a dragoon regiment and, whilst the Spanish had Gibraltar under siege, he left the Madrid court, going first to Bayonne and then to Paris where, in April 1727, he

---

[1]　BL: Stowe MS256, pp70-71. Letter from Newcastle to Stanhope, dated 22nd December 1726

(along with Horace Walpole Senior) had a favourable audience with Louis XV. From Paris he journeyed to Dover and a return to England.

Within a short time, there was new King as George II succeeded his father and that year William was asked to join the Privy Council and William worked well with the new King with whom he had a common approach - being more in favour of war than the cautious Walpole and Newcastle.

Another appointment followed as Vice Lord Chamberlain of the Household in 1727-30, which was perhaps a symbol of his favouritism as it was a high office at court. In this post William held a trusted position within the royal household and he could control those individuals appointed to serve the sovereign at the various royal establishments. Beyond that, the post involved having control of all state ceremonials; including coronations, funerals, marriages etc down to the more mundane matters such as licensing of plays and drama.

Before leaving England on more diplomatic missions, William had himself elected to parliament as MP for Steyning and Derby. William Stanhope's extensive experience at the European courts, in particular with Spain, made his involvement at the Conferences of Aix-la-Chapelle and Soissons inevitable, indeed essential.

Horace Walpole, brother to Prime Minister Walpole, led the delegation (which included Martin Bladen of the Board of Trade) that attended a series of meetings designed to smooth out any differences between Britain and Spain and, although not considered a complete success, Soissons did go some way to reduce tensions, at least until the next flare up between the nations over Jenkins' Ear. William was one of the signators to the Treaty of Seville on 9th November 1729 which effectively concluded the Anglo-Spanish War.

In 1730, Newcastle discussed his desire to see Stanhope with a peerage which saw William created Baron Harrington (of Harrington, Northampton) from 6th January 1730/31, though there is no record of him having actually spoken in the House of Lords. It was also at this time that William began a relationship with Anne Vane, a maid of honour at court. The wedding was notified in the Evening Post but never took place, though Anne is thought to have become William's mistress. Described as "a promiscuous woman",[1] Anne gave birth to a son in 1732 who she called Fitz Frederick Vane and she claimed paternity belonged to Frederick, Prince of Wales. Other names in the frame were John Hervey, 2nd Baron Hervey and William Stanhope himself.

Shortly after his peerage he was once again

---

[1]   Libertines and Harlots by Norman Milne

despatched to another conference in France and was also being discussed as a successor to Lord Townshend as Secretary of State for the North. This development, when confirmed, saw him return to England on 18th June 1730.

The skills which made William such an accomplished diplomat seemed to infuriate some. Horace Walpole, writing to Harrington in 1735, said *"I am very sensible that your good breeding and naturall disposition can't help being civill to ye De--ll if he waited upon you"*.[1] By the same token the Queen was said to dislike Harrington, stating *"there is a heavy insipid sloth in that man that puts me out of all patience"*[2] and her poor opinion may have affected the King's enthusiasm for him, which dimmed in later years.

In the later 1730s Britain was, yet again, braced for impending war with Spain and Stanhope allied himself more with Newcastle's slightly harder line, as opposed to Walpole's reluctance to engage in an expensive war. After Townshend's death Stanhope was appointed Secretary of State for the Northern Department by April 1730. At the same time, Stanhope was becoming increasingly concerned about his personal finances. Like

---

[1]   Lewis Walpole Library, Yale University, Weston MSS Vol. 2. Walpole's letter to Harrington dated 20th October 1735 n.s.
[2]   Hervey, 2.346

many other ambassadors overseas, Stanhope found his finances under a strain as the status of his job required a certain standard of living which was difficult to maintain. He brought the matter to the King's attention in June 1740 and sought an appointment as Teller of the Exchequer to rescue his finances. He was made President of the Privy Council.

In 1740 a poem was published by Elizabeth Boyd addressed to William, called "Truth, A Poem" of which the following are extracts:-[1]

> Stanhope the Good, the Gen'rous, and the Just,
> Dear to his Prince, and faithful to his Trust,
> Of Friends, of Patriots, and of Men the best.
> ... Whilst Godlike Harrington, in Perilso old,
> As Virtue steady, and as Honour bold,
> Unaw'd surveys the scaulking Privateer,
> Stranger to Baseness, and as new to Fear,
> Nor bulky Fleets, nor thund'ring Cannon Scare;
> Tho' fraudful France, with coward Spaine unite,
> Maugre their substile, ill-concerted spite,
> Triumphant, the victorius Briton glows
> And unconcerned, quells such inglorious Foes.

Following Walpole's departure from office, Stanhope was given an Earldom in February 1742 and he stepped down as Secretary of State. In 1743 he was appointed Lord Justice (Regent) during the King's absence in

---

[1]   In 1740 William had a poem written "Truth, A Poem" Addressed to the Right Honourable William Lord Harrington by Elizabeth Boyd.

Hanover for almost one year. When his replacement, Lord Carteret left office after a short tenure, Stanhope was once again returned to being a Secretary of State in 1744 but his attitude, particularly to the King's Hanoverian interests, had markedly changed and by February 1746 he relinquished the post on the issue of policy, resigning just before Newcastle. From this point onwards, Stanhope was well and truly out of favour.

In August of that year his eldest son William married Lady Caroline Fitzroy, daughter of Charles Fitzroy, 2nd Duke of Grafton.

His career, however, was not quite over as he obtained an appointment as Lord Lieutenant of Ireland to replace his relative Lord Chesterfield who had been moved to become Secretary of State. The robust style of politics in Ireland, however, did not suit the polite and ever courteous diplomat who was increasingly suffering with the gout. His political career faded away after his spell in Ireland and died December 1756.

Severns

Whilst those Stanhopes charged with possession of the estate at Elvaston were busily serving their country overseas or attending Parliament or their princes at Court, management of their Derbyshire estate rested with others. This small section will look at one family who spent all their time at Elvaston and who were, at least initially, in service to the noble Stanhopes.

When walking through the churchyard of St Bartholomew's Church at Elvaston, you cannot help but notice the abundance of gravestones for members of the Severn family. They line a section of the main path from the church to nearby Elvaston Castle and the family members were all connected in some way with the Stanhopes and the estate of the Earls of Harrington.

For well over 150 years there were generations of Severns living and working in the small hamlet of Elvaston but there appear to be no descendants living today and all trace of them has gone.

The lives of a few members of the Severn family mentioned in this chapter were just as closely connected with Elvaston Castle and day to day life there, even if their circumstances were more humble.

SEVERN FAMILY TREE

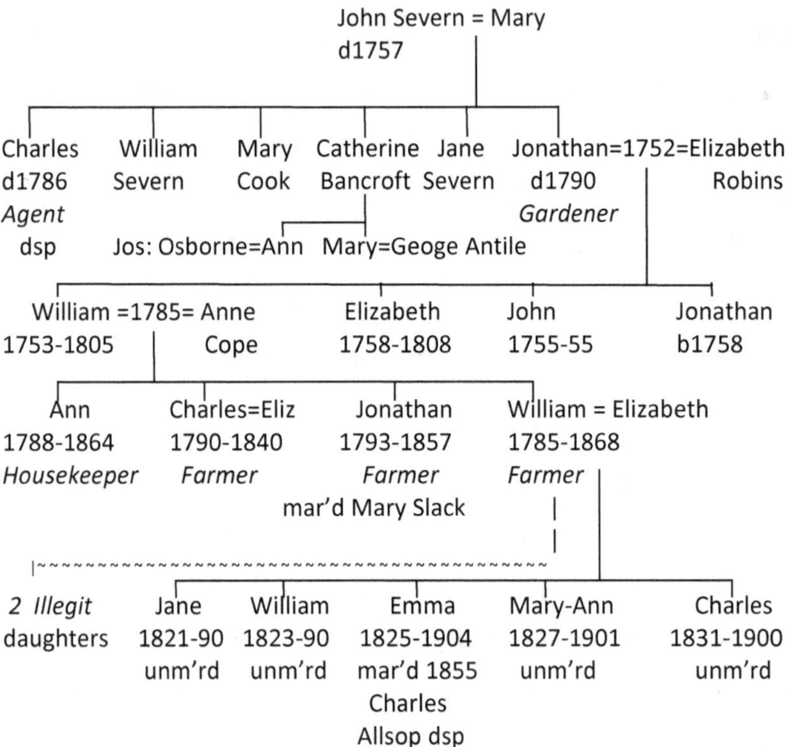

The first Severns who appear in records connected with the Stanhope's estate at Elvaston were Agents for the family. They held land, either by purchase or lease from the Stanhopes, and were reasonably prosperous and well thought of by the Lord of the Manor.

JOHN SEVERN d1757

John, one of many generations of Severns who went by that Christian name, was the first who appears in documents dating as far back as 1711. He was named in land transactions concerning Thomas Stanhope 1680-1743, whose youngest brother would later become 1st Earl of Harrington.

The Stanhopes had good need for agents and stewards to organise their extensive land holdings, to liaise with their tenants in numerous counties as well as collecting rents and keeping their holdings rented out and generating income.

John married Mary and the couple had six children; three boys and three girls. Sons Charles and Jonathan became steward and gardener respectively to Charles Stanhope (brother of the 1st Earl of Harrington) then continued working for succeeding Earls. These jobs were very much 'for life' and, once appointed, generation after generation stayed, either being employed by the estate or renting their farms and land from the Stanhopes.

After the death of Thomas, Lord of the Manor, John Severn continued his service to the Stanhopes and was employed until his own death in 1757 by the brother Charles.

Severn's Will showed him as having houses and land at Draycott, which he rented out and he also received interest from Thomas Robins of Elvaston who held a mortgage on another of Severn's properties. Five years before John died, the daughter of Thomas Robins would marry John's own son in 1752 at Elvaston.

John died in 1757 and divided his estate principally between his two sons Charles and Jonathan as well as small legacies to his son William and daughters Mary Cook, Catherine Bancroft[1] and Jane Severn.

CHARLES SEVERN 1786

Charles Severn, eldest son of John above, seems to have followed in his father's footsteps being engaged by the Stanhopes.[2] From the reference to him and his family in bachelor Charles Stanhope's Will of 1760, the Severns were very well thought of: *"I give to Charles Severn my Steward £100 and to his brother and sister who live with me at my house at Elvaston £40 apiece and to Mrs Catherine Severn and to her two daughters £40 apiece."*

---

[1]   Catherine Bancroft had two daughters, referred to in the notes appended to Charles Severn's Will: being Anne, wife of Joseph Osborne and Mary wife of George Antile. Joseph Osborne was maltster to the Earl of Harrington

[2]   DRO: D518/ME/121, Auction particulars of estate at Bingham and Blidworth, Nottinghamshire, including Manor of Heywood, agent Charles Severn of Elvaston, dated 1779

As Stanhope spent much of his life attending parliament, his agent Charles Severn would have been closely trusted to manage the Elvaston estate. Charles Stanhope, writing in his Will, made mention of the Severns residing with him at his home, by which it is presumed he meant that they resided nearby – perhaps in the buildings in the courtyard due west of the main castle. The younger brother of Charles Severn (about to be discussed) is referred to in later documents as the earl's gardener and, since there is a gardener's cottage showing on estate maps immediately next to what was a one-time real tennis court and the stables, then this seems the likely location for the Severns to have resided.

Stanhope, who outlived both of his brothers, was succeeded by his nephew, William 2nd Earl of Harrington, who he made his principal heir in his Will and William Stanhope moved in to Elvaston Castle with his wife Caroline Fitzroy and their children.

Charles Severn probably knew little or nothing about William Stanhope, the new Earl and his family. Countess Caroline, who was called one of the 'Beauty Fitzoys' was said to live a licentious lifestyle. So too did her husband the Earl who was called, rather cruelly by Horace Walpole, 'Peter Shambles' due to his eccentric appearance of a twisted nose and legs. The couple spent much of their time living at their London home rather than Elvaston.

The 2nd Earl of Harrington died before Charles Severn and there would have been yet another change of ownership at the castle. The 3rd Earl of Harrington, however, was a notably different character to his father and his occupancy of Elvaston heralded a long period of stability of ownership lasting several decades. When Charles Severn died in 1786, he left his estate to his nephew William, son of his younger brother Jonathan, with smaller legacies to other nieces and friends. His brother was one of the witnesses to the Will.

JONATHAN SEVERN d1790

Jonathan Severn, brother of the above Charles, outlived his brother by just four years. He was likewise in the employ of Charles Stanhope, and by 1772 he had become the 2nd earl's gardener, at which time he took out a 21 year lease on land from the earl as follows:

Derbyshire Record Office: D518/ME/34, 1772
William, Earl of Harrington [2nd]
21 year lease to Jonathan Severn of Elvaston, the Earl's Gardener of 57 acres of the paddock, 1 rood at Foster's Yard, 30 Perches at The Croft, the intake between the Plantations, 3 acres 1 rood at Ley Close, 30 perches in Elvaston and cottage in Boulton with 2 acres 1 rood in Alvaston Meadow (2 acres, 1 rood) for £29 per annum with £5 per acre ploughed pasture.

The location of Jonathan's leased land can be identified as The Paddock which is a short distance away from the Gardener's Cottage previously mentioned. The area of land he leased was in the same general locale, that is beyond the stables to the west of the castle, between the castle and Home Farm. The Intake referred to in his lease was either a parcel of land taken in from Boulton Moor and brought into cultivation, or, a reference to it being near the top end of the serpentine lake where water was taken in, then flowed out at the bottom of the lake to a water wheel which pumped water from an adjacent well into a water tower at the castle.

Unlike his bachelor brother Charles, Jonathan married. On 10 Jan 1752 he married at Elvaston to Elizabeth Robins, a daughter of Thomas Robins mentioned in the Will of Charles Severn above. Her father, who left her £100 when he died, had borrowed money against a property from John Severn senior. Jonathan Junior and Elizabeth had four children and the expansion of his family may have prompted his leasing the messuage in Boulton (Alvaston) in the above lease on the Harrington's estate, to accommodate his burgeoning family.   It was still on Harrington lands but would have placed him out of the castle's immediate vicinity.

Of their four children, two appear to have died as

infants.   Daughter Elizabeth did not marry and son William was to be the one who continued the line.

WILLIAM SEVERN 1753-1805

Said son William 1753-1805 married on Christmas Eve 24th December 1785 in Sandiacre to Anne Cope and they also had four children.   He must have inherited his father's property at Alvaston/Boulton as his name occurs on the 1798 UK Land Tax Redemption records as follows:-

UK Land Tax Redemption, 1798
Proprietor: Earl of Harrington
Residence: Liberty of Alvaston and Boulton, Derby, England
An Assessment made in pursuance of an Act of
Parliament passed in the 38th year of His Majesty's
Reign, for granting an aid to His Majesty by a Land Tax to
be raised in Great Britain for the service of the year 1798

Name of Proprietor: Earl of Harrington
Name of Owner: Wm Briggs
Sum assessed: 12 shillings

Name of Proprietor: Earl of Harrington
Name of Owner: Wm Severn
Sum assessed: 9 shillings[1]

---

[1]   Other records show: UK Land Tax Redemption, 1798, Long Eaton. No. of register: Earl of Harrington Proprietor, Occupier Chief: 3s 6d. Earl of Harrington, occupier Jno: Raynor, 6s; UK Land Tax Redemption, 1798.

William also seems to have continued the family tradition of working for the Earls of Harrington as documents from 1792-98 show him collecting rents for the estate.[1]

William died intestate and his widow Anne managed to outlive him by some thirty years. Little more is known about William except that he must have held and consolidated his inherited wealth as his sons both had farms. Wife Anne died in 1836[2] and on 12th April that year her eldest son William took responsibility for administering her estate which was valued at less than £450.

William seems to have been the last of the Severns who were actively working for the Stanhope family. Two of his sons were tenants of the family throughout their lives but, so far as is known, they were farming in their own right and for their own benefit rather than working for the estate.

Hundred of Morleston and Litchurch; Proprietor: Earl of Harrington; Liberty of Wilstrop (Wilsthorpe), Derby; Proprietor: Earl of Harrington, tenant Tho: Sheldon £3-2-2.5d; Proprietor: Earl of Harrington, tenant Wlm Harriman £2-14-2.5d; Proprietor: Earl of Harrington, tenant Jno: Rayner £3-17-6d; Proprietor: Earl of Harrington, tenant Tho: Theobald £1-9-4d; Proprietor: Earl of Harrington, tenant Wlm Brentnall £1-2s-10.5d

[1]   DRO: D5336/2/23/109 'Account of chief rents paid to Mr Severn (for Lord Harrington) and paid to Mr Severn for Daffodilly Meadow', 1792-98
[2]   Letters of Administration 1836 for Anne Severn

WILLIAM SEVERN 1785-1868

William, son of the above, led a more colourful life than his father. Starting with the birth of two illegitimate children; the first born on 9th February 1816 to Lucy Bourne[1] and the second 18 months later on 22nd October 1817,[2] an infant called Louisa to Elizabeth Longman[3] and both cited William Severn as the father on the subsequent bastardy bonds that were issued. William would have been obligated to pay maintenance money to the churchwarden or overseer of the poor until the children were of an age to go into an apprenticeship. In the case of the Longman infant he was in bond for £200. If he failed to do this and the children became a burden on the parish, he could be sent to prison.

William was in business farming with his brother and they had wagons painted 'Jonathan and William Severn' which were a familiar sight around the village. Although William was the eldest, perhaps brother Jonathan owning three-times the size of farm gave him seniority in name placing.

William married Elizabeth Chadwick (1799-1851) in

---

[1]   DRO: D5717 Bastardy Maintenance Bonds, 1816

[2]   DRO: D2081/A/PO/5/1Bastardy Maintenance Bonds, 1817

[3]   Elizabeth Longman was born 1794 to an Elvaston family: 4 sisters, 1 brother. Daughter Louisa Longman was born 1st June 1817 at Elvaston

1820 at All Saints Church, Derby.[1] Elizabeth died aged 52 years at Elvaston, just a few weeks before the 1851 census which duly showed William, now widowed, farming 53 acres and living with his unmarried children. Ten years later the land acres have reduced to 23 and so have the dependent children.

For reasons which will become apparent, it is likely that William dominated his younger brother Jonathan and, in respect of his brother's estate, he seems to gone to considerable lengths to prevent his brother's house and land going to others when he died.

Their sister Ann 1788-1864 remained a spinster and she kept house for her brothers. In her Will, Ann left her interest in farming stock to the value of £250 to her nephew Charles (son of her brother William), with the remainder of her personal estate being divided between her nieces Jane and Mary Ann, also children of her brother William. Effects under £300.

Another sibling Charles 1790-1840 kept a farm in nearby Alvaston (Boulton) and, although he married Elizabeth, the couple had no children and, after his death in 1840, Elizabeth remarried.

All three sons; William, Jonathan and Charles were listed

---

[1]   Staffordshire, Dioceses of Lichfield & Coventry marriage allegations and bonds, 1636-1893. Occupation Farmer, residence parish Thurlston

in the Derby Election of 1835, Southern Division, where their votes were recorded on 20th & 21st January of that year. The candidates were Sir Roger Gresley, Sir George Crew, Hon. G.J. Vernon and Rt. Hon. Lord Waterpark and all three Severn brothers voted for Sir Roger Gresley and Sir George Crewe.

William Severn d1868

William described himself as a gentleman in his Will of 1862 and his list of assets show him to have become a man of some means. He described his home as being located at the Croft and Match Flat Closes at Elvaston, containing about 15 acres in addition, of course, to his farmhouse and outbuildings. These premises were devised to his eldest son William though charged with an annuity of £10 p.a. to his daughter Mary Ann. In addition William had more lands called the 'New Close' adjoining the Borrowash Lane containing 7 acres, 3 roods and 26 perches which he bequeathed to his second son Charles. In a similar fashion he charged this with an annuity of £10 to daughter Jane.

His sister Ann had an interest of £250 in the estate devised to William for her life time which, in her own Will, Ann reverts to William (the son).[1] In money terms, William gave his two unmarried daughters Jane and Mary Ann £200 each and to his two sons £500 each and such sums were to be invested in public stocks or funds, also he included a sum for married daughter Emma Allsop.

Interestingly William also had shares in Sawley Bridge, which is elsewhere in this book called 'Harrington Bridge', being constructed by the 3rd Earl across the River Trent near Sawley. As it was a toll bridge when first completed, William and others would have had good reasons to purchase shares in it which would have rendered them exempt from the toll fee. His shares were divided between his two unmarried daughters. Effects under £1,000.[2]

---

[1]   DRO: Will of Ann Severn, 1865, I.D. 122, M254

JONATHAN SEVERN 1793-1857

The youngest son Jonathan appears to have been a very successful farmer of 154 acres, employing four agricultural labourers at one time. Through all of the census returns he stated his marital status to be single, even in the 1851 census - which was the last one before his death, which was not, in fact, true. He had gone through a wedding ceremony with Mary Slack on 4th December 1850 at Kennington in Surrey, claiming himself to be a Labourer residing at Church Street. Probably he had been required to attend London on behalf of the Earl of Harrington because the Severns were not known to have any particular connection with Kennington on their own behalf:-

MARRIAGE took place on 4th December 1850
at St Mark's, Kennington, Surrey, England
Between Jonathan Severn, Labourer,
Church Street son of William Severn, and
Mary Slack daughter of Thomas Slack of Kennington, Surrey

Miss Slack, however, had strong ties to Elvaston and had a nephew living there. Slack relations were living at Elvaston Lodge where a John Slack was gardener and sexton at Elvaston. Other relations were butchers in the

---

[2]   DRO: Will of William Severn, 1868, I.D. 922, M257

village and, they far out-numbered Severns in the locality. Immediately after the marriage, his new wife claimed, she was told to remove her wedding ring and her new husband abandoned her in London and returned to Elvaston. Mary followed him and her story was recorded in a law suit for her maintenance which followed.

George Slack, a labourer residing at Elvaston brought an action, Slack v Severne, against Jonathan Severne, farmer at Elvaston to recover the sum of £4-10s for maintaining the defendant's wife. Mr Briggs represented Slack the Plaintiff and Mr Borough represented the defendant.

Recorded as Mary Slack, however, rather than Mary Severn, the 1851 census shows Mary's presence in Elvaston with her nephew George (son of William Slack and Maria Thorpe - married 24 November 1817, Elvaston). William and Thomas Slack were farmers and butchers at Elvaston.

The 1851 Census shows the situation, residence Elvaston Street

George Slack	Head	age 30	Born Elvaston occupation: gardener
Mary Slack	Wife	age 33	Born Meriden, Warks
William Slack	Son	age 2	Born Elvaston
Samuel Slack	Son	age 1	Born Elvaston
Mira Slack	Sister	age 21	Born Elvaston
Mary Slack	**Aunt**	**age 39**	**Born Elvaston**

Outline: Mrs Severn lived in a cottage at Elvaston, the rent of which had been formerly paid by her husband. He, however, had abandoned her; and the plaintiff (Slack) who lived nearby in a cottage, and who had a wife and five children, had compassion on her and, for several months past, has been maintaining her. Slack brought the action against Severn, a wealthy farmer, to compel him to return to him the amount he had expended on his wife. The defendant's sisters, Misses Severn, would not allow her to enter their house and she had not resided with her husband for years.

George Slack: I am nephew to Mrs Severne, who married Jonathan Severne, farmer, Elvaston, several years ago. Jonathan Severne lives with his sisters. I produce a copy of the Elvaston ratebook showing that he is rated at between £200 and £300. He used to allow my aunt £6 a year to live on, but she has not received any money from him since the first week in September. His sisters will not allow him to acknowledge his wife, and when she goes to ask to see him the door is shut in her face. In September last she was perfectly destitute, with scarcely a rag on her back, and I gave her 6s to go and buy a gown with; and I have also found her in food since that time. She has four meals a day at my house, and is welcome to six a day if she could eat them. Two of my children sleep with Mrs Severne at her cottage.

His Honour:　　　Very natural.

George Slack:　　She does not do my work. I don't know that defendant lives with his brother William Severne. I know that he rents a house under Lord Harrington.

Mrs Severne:　　I was married several years ago to the defendant, Jonathan Severne, in the district of Kennington, London. I produce a copy of my marriage certificate. After I was married to him he made me take my wedding-ring off, and left me in London. I followed him to Elvaston, when he wished the wedding to be kept a secret, and I lived four years with my nephew. During that time I spent £40 which I had saved whilst in service, to maintain myself with. He never maintained me nor lived with me, and his sisters would not allow me to enter his own house. He is a man of property, and when I married him the stock on the farm was all his own. He is joint tenant of the farm with his brother William Severne. He promised to allow me £10 a year, but has not done so. In September last, I was destitute of clothing, and my nephew advanced me 6s to purchase a gown with. The only debt I ever contracted in my husband's name was 11s-8d for some bread when I was starving, and in consequence of application being made to him for that amount his friends put an advertisement in one of the Derby papers cautioning people not to trust me, and stating that I was not his wife. I put an advertisement in the paper the week following stating that I was his wife, and also stating where the marriage took place. The advertisement they put in the paper was a wilful mis-statement of facts. The small account for bread is the only debt that

I have contracted since I have been married.

My husband has not been an imbecile for the last ten years. Mr William Severne paid me 2s-6d a week for nine weeks. My husband has £900 worth of property at Draycott.

I have several times tried to see my husband, but his sisters will not let me enter the house.

William Severn: The defendant resides with me. He has spent all his money, having been a man of very drunken habits. I am tenant of the farm, and produce the receipt of rent paid by me to Mr Curzon, Lord Harrington's steward. Defendant is not joint tenant with me. At the death of my brother he became possessed of one-third of the personalty, but he has spent that amount over and over again. Out of charity I have given his wife 2s-6d a week for several weeks. If I turned him out of the house he would have to go to the Union.

Mr Jones: (Surgeon) Deposed that he had attended defendant for several years past: he had an attack of paralysis. Mr William Severne paid him for his attendance, and he believed he was the owner of the farm.

Mr Briggs: (Solicitor for Plaintiff): Mr Jones, have you never observed on the carts and wagons the names of "Jonathan and William Severn"?

Mr Jones: I believe I have.

George Slack: Yes, your Honor, and they have painted the word "Jonathan" out since the present action has been brought.

His Honour: Is that a fact?

George Slack: It is, your Honor.

His Honour: If the name has been altered within the last fortnight an attempt at fraud has been practiced. This is an instance in which a drunken man goes to London, persuades a woman to marry him, brings her to his home, she is not acknowledged by his family, and then he is persuaded to abandon her. Having married her he was bound to maintain her in the same sphere of life in which he was himself. If he was in the station of life that had been represented, he considered the claim of 8s per week a reasonable one. If he was only a lodger with his brother, how was it that he was on the rate-book of 11th November 1856 for the large sum of £256-5s?

He should give a verdict for the plaintiff for the full amount to be paid forthwith.[1]

One year later, Jonathan Severn was dead and a brand new Court of Probate Act had been introduced and the Severns were to be the first case examined in Derby under the new law. The same lawyers represented the same clients and wife Mary was the defendant. The case rested on what was Jonathan's state of mind when he wrote his Will; his first Will having left a small maintenance to his wife, but the final Will disinherited her completely. Mary's counsel challenged probate because she felt the Will was made under 'undue influence'; that is to say Jonathan's brother William had taken advantage of Jonathan's drunkenness and imbecile state to write the Will for him and have Jonathan merely sign it. It was the same judge who had found in Mary's favour the year before.

---

[1] Derbyshire Advertiser and Journal, 20th February 1857: Slack v Severne. Derby County Court Monday Feb 16th before J.T. Cantrell

His Honour: (to Mary's Counsel) On what ground do you oppose?

Briggs: On the grounds of imbecility, arising from old age and drunkenness, of undue influence, and on the general grounds attending such circumstances. *Mr Eason of the District Probate Court produced the Will.*

Witnesses were called who confirmed the Will was written on the day as stated, 31st January 1857 and executed in the presence of Mr Jones of Shardlow, Surgeon.

Mr Curzon: (Solicitor, Full Street, Derby) claimed he had known the deceased for 40 years, knew he was unwell. On arriving at the plaintiff's house where William gave Curzon instructions for writing the Will. Plaintiff told him to leave 5*l.* to testator's wife and his household furniture in her possession etc. After writing out the Will, Curzon took it to Jonathan Severn's house and Mr Jones, surgeon, came in where they found the deceased sitting by the fire, perfectly sober and the deceased's sister and family were there. The Will was read over to him (deceased) and he assented and signed it. His hand was too shaky for him to write and he made his mark. Deceased understood what the paper was. Curzon said 'It is a common practice, as every solicitor knows, to prepare a Will from the instructions of a third person, without seeing the testator and reading it over to him after it was prepared.'

His Honour:	Am I to understand that this is really the practice of solicitors? If so, it is a very objectionable one.
Curzon:	I have done it many times.
His Honour:	The duty of a solicitor, before he makes a Will is to see the testator himself, and take instructions from him. To ask him what property he has, who are his relations, and in what way he wishes to dispose of his property.
Mr Borough:	He expressed himself perfectly satisfied and said that was his wish.

Michael Thomas Jones Esq of Shardlow, surgeon, was then examined and said he had been in the habit of attending the late Mr Jonathan Severn for 25 or 30 years. In May 1856, he was seized with paralysis, from which attack he suffered to the time of his death. He attested the Will, and after it had been read over to deceased he (witness) asked him if he understood it, and whether it was by his wife, and he said yes. It was then executed by him in the presence of witness and Mr Wheatcroft. But after he executed the Will witness took it up and said, Do you know this is your Will, and he said Yes? His mind was weakened and his body was weakened to a great extent, but not so far as to prevent him from knowing what he was about. When questions were put to him he answered properly, but was never disposed to conversation. He was anxious before to make a new will.

Briggs: (Cross examined witness) when he further stated that deceased knew he had a wife, but had never had her with him. When before the magistrates in December 1856, a month before the Will was made he (witness) said deceased was incapable of coming to Derby - he was partially imbecile, and would become totally so if he was subjected to the excitement of coming to Derby. He could not say that he did not then say the deceased had been imbecile for six months. Any little thing alarmed him, and he was constantly afraid of his wife coming. His sister was exceedingly kind to him. He sometimes said he was married and sometimes said he was not, but if he had been it was when he was drunk, for he had not the slightest recollection of it. His mind constantly wandered. Drink had been the cause of his affliction. He was about sixty years of age at his death. He alluded to his Will afterwards. He said before that he had nothing to leave. In this court he (witness) had said deceased was partially imbecile.

On re-examination witness stated that he attended deceased daily, or nearly so. On one or two occasions, he said he had done with his wife.

His Honour: Suppose you had asked him how he wished to dispose of his property, could he have said?

Jones: I think he could have done at that time. At a conversation deceased expressed a wish to me to alter his Will in consequence of his wife's conduct. In the second Will he wished to leave her nothing; in the first he had left her 5s a week

Henry Gisborne: (Derby surgeon) Stated that early in March last, he met Mr Jones at deceased's house and was left to ask deceased questions. He (witness) perceived that deceased was weak in mind and body, but he was quite prepared to give an answer to a simple question, and he afterwards found his answers were truthful. The questions put to him were respecting the fame and other matters of business. He said the farm was not his.

His Honour: If he had been asked could he have said how he wished to dispose of his property?

Mr Gisborne:	I think that doubtful. If a person had gone to him and proposed a plain question to him he could have answered it, but I think he would have had a difficulty in directing that.
Rev. Highmore	(Vicar of Elvaston) said he was acquainted with the deceased first about 25 years ago, and was always in the habit of calling upon him, and must have seen him very shortly before the Will was made, and he saw him about two hours before his death. He (witness) conversed with him, and put the plainest questions in the plainest way, and he always gave reasonable answers. He never found him insane or incompetent, but was feeble of mind and body. On cross-examination witness also said that he went to pray by deceased. Until latterly he was more frequent up than in bed. Whether he knew him (witness) on one occasion he (witness) could not say. He frequently fell asleep; when witness understood that deceased knew, he read and prayed to him. He at times alluded to his wife, and spoke of her ill behaviour to him.

Once he said she was no wife of his, but witness understood him to mean that she had not behaved like a wife to him.

Borough: When deceased spoke of his wife he appeared to be speaking of his own feelings.

Rev. James Jones: (Curate of Elvaston), said he became acquainted with deceased the first week in January 1857, when he called on him as he did on all parishioners on his arrival at Elvaston as curate. He saw him once, twice, or three times a week. His mind was weak but conscious, and he gave reasonable answers to plain and simple questions. He (witness) should have thought he was competent to make a Will. He asked him whether he was willing to give up a house then in the occupation of his wife, and he said yes. On seeing his wife come to the window and rap at it several times, he became pallid. On cross-examination witness said he never saw deceased transact business.

His Honour: He assented; did he ever dissent?

Mr Jones:	I do no remember that he did. I asked him to whom I must pay the money in respect of the fixtures in that house, and he said Keep it. I understood this to mean that I was to keep it for the present.

Mr Highmore was here recalled, and said that he was told deceased that the proper person to nurse him was his wife, and that he would soon leave this world, and it was his duty to make peace with all. He answered that he wished to do all that was right, but he could not be reconciled.

His Honour:	Directed that Will to be read.

This concluded the Plaintiff's case.

Briggs:	Addressed the court and contended that the evidence for the plaintiff proved that the deceased was imbecile, and therefore not capable of making a Will. He then cited from a digest by Halilay which stated that 'mental imbecility occasioned by great age or drunkenness will incapacitate a man from making a will'. He also cited from a note to Blackstone's Commentaries by Hovenden, pointing out what

amounted to a lucid interval within the meaning of the law so as to entitle a party to make a Will, in which Sir William Wynne, in the case of Cartwright v Cartwright, 1 Phill. 100, said if it be shown that the party did what is a rational act, and that it was his own act entirely, nothing is left to presumption in order to prove a lucid interval; but unquestionably there must be a complete and absolute proof that the party did the act (of which the validity is in question) without any assistance'. He then commended on the evidence for the plaintiff, and contended that if deceased had been so far restored as to enable him to have gone about his business, there would have been a restoration, but such was not the case; there was, therefore, no pretence on that ground for saying deceased was able to make his Will. He then remarked on the fact of the plaintiff Mr William Severn, who had given the instructions for the Will and had performed so prominent a part in the matter, not having been called.

Mrs Severn: (widow of deceased). Stated she was married on 4th December 1850 at Kennington Church, London. Before that she lived in his house as his servant. He left her in London and afterwards sent for her but, when she came, he did not take her to his own home for fear of his relations. She had some money of her own at her marriage, which she afterwards spent on her maintenance. In September last she went to see her husband and he did not know her. He seemed quite out of his mind. He said if he met her he should not know her, she was not his wife, and they had not been married, and he did not remember going to London. On another occasion he said she had stolen all the watches and bottles that were in the house. A short time afterwards she asked him for money and he said she had plenty of money, she had been round with Mr Highmore collecting. She spoke to Mr Highmore several times, and once he said that he could not get deceased to say that he would see his wife, his mind wandered, he was going to London and all over the world.   He said he did not think deceased was himself.   This was November   1856.   Before   the magistrates Mr Jones, surgeon, said the deceased was an imbecile and had been from the May before. The magistrates asked Mr Jones whether deceased knew that he was married, and Mr Jones said he had heard him say that he was and that he was not. The plaintiff and his sister fed and dressed deceased, and he dare not say anything or do anything except under them.   When she (witness) went up stairs to her husband, three or four of his brother's family followed her. [Several letters from deceased to his wife were produced, and one of them read.]

Ellen Shaw: (Late servant to plaintiff) said that in October 1856 deceased sometimes told her to fetch Mary, meaning his wife, and when his wife came he would not speak to her. She (witness) thought he was not in his own mind. Sometimes he would not eat.

Charles Baker of Elvaston (farmer) and George Slack of Elvaston were called to prove that Mr Jones, surgeon, stated to the magistrates that deceased was an imbecile.

Mr Stone:	Stated that in April 1857 he applied to Mr William Severn the plaintiff for maintenance of his wife, and Mr Severn afterwards called on him and said he was willing to allow her 5s a week; his brother was a pauper, and if proceedings were taken he must go to the union. By drinking he had brought on imbecility.
His Honour:	Questions were: was the deceased of disposing mind? Was he allowed to exercise it? This is an important question, the first in this court under the Probate Act. It is an application to have probate granted of the Will of the late Jonathan Severn. The Will appears to have been executed in proper form, and by that Will the testator appointed his brother William his executor and he now makes the present application, which is opposed on the part of Mary Severn, the widow of the testator, on the ground that the testator was not competent to make a Will and that he was unduly influenced. The bulk of the evidence was on the part of Mr William

Severn; the defendant's evidence amounts to little, and it was not likely to be much, as those who had access to the testator were brought on the part of the plaintiff. What are the circumstances then? The Will appears to have been executed in proper form, and is prepared by Mr Wheatcroft, who stated that he has known deceased for forty years but who had not seen him for some time before the execution of the Will. The brother sends for him and he takes instructions from the brother at his brother's house and writes the Will clearly out and takes it and reads if over to Mr Jonathan Severn, and asks him to sign it. It is said that this is the practice of solicitors frequently. If it be, I cannot use language too strong to express my disapprobation of it, and if I give judgment against the Will I shall be mainly influenced by that circumstance. The practice is a most improper one and, whenever it is resorted to, it will afford the strong ground on the part of the parties interested to impeach that Will. If the person had gone to the deceased and put his questions as a lawyer, and asked what property he had to dispose of and how did he wish to dispose of it - did he wish to give his wife or his brother anything, and what? Which would have been the proper mode - and he had given reasonable and intelligent answers, and then gone and written the Will, there would have been very strong grounds for coming here. As regards the state of the deceased's mind Mr Jones admitted that he had represented him as partially imbecile and weak in body and mind, and other witnesses said the representation was that he was totally imbecile. There is no evidence that deceased had given a denial. A person of weak mind very often will not give himself the trouble to deny, and will therefore assent to whatever is asked of him.

Borough: Your Honour will pardon me calling your attention to Mr Highmore's evidence that he refused to be reconciled to his wife.

His Honour: Did not consider that a denial within his meaning. The deceased told Mr Jones that he wished to leave nothing to his wife but that is not the Will. As regards the competency of the deceased to make a Will, there is the evidence of Mr Jones that he was, and Mr Gisborne said he put plain questions and he answered them reasonably, but when I asked Mr Gisborne whether he was able to give instructions he hesitated, and said he did not think his mind was equal to that. Both Mr Jones and Mr Gisborne say he was very weak in body and mind. But the clergymen stated that they merely put simple questions easily comprehensible, such as they always did in such cases, that he was able to give satisfactory answers to them, and appeared to feel his position. Does that lead to the inference that he had a willing and disposing mind, and was allowed to exercise it? Looking at all evidence, particularly at the way in which the Will was made, I am led to the conclusion that the Will is the Will of Mr William and not the Will of Mr Jonathan Severn, and that Jonathan Severn signed it under undue influence. I therefore come to the conclusion the plaintiff is not entitled to probate on the ground that the deceased Jonathan Severn was a person of weak and feeble mind, and was unduly influenced by the plaintiff in making his Will.

Briggs:

Applied for costs, which his Honour granted.[1]

In Memory of the late Johnathan Severn who died October 31st 1857 aged 57 years. And of Ann Severn, sister of the above, who died December 13th, 1864 aged 77 years. St Bartholomew's Churchyard, Elvaston. The dates on the grave stones are a little 'out'.[2]

---

[1]   County Court Chronicle, 1st June 1858

CHILDREN OF WILLIAM SEVERN 1787-1868

Eldest daughter Jane 1821-1890, died 14th January 1890, unmarried:

WILLIAM SEVERN 1823-90

Eldest son William was a farmer and, on the 1871

---

[2]   1835: List of electors for the southern division of the county of Derby showing how they voted at the contested election, 20th & 21st January 1835:
     Candidates: Sir Roger Gresley, Sir George Crewe, Hon G.J. Vernon, Rt. Hon Lord Waterpark. All three brothers Jonathan, William and Charles all voted for Sir Roger Gresley and Sir George Crewe

census, was recorded as farming 23 acres, which is a surprisingly small sum compared to his younger brother who was farming 183 acres. Their father had died in 1868 so it would have been expected that his estate would be divided perhaps more or less equally between the two sons, or even more in favour of the elder. He had his sister Mary Ann, unmarried, living with him.

Ten years later and another census shows William still farming the same 23 acres, though now employing one man. He also had his three sisters with him; the two unmarried ones as well as Emma, the now widowed sister.

William died on 29th July 1890 at Elvaston and his Will of 1889 left his personal and real estate to his younger brother Charles. Gross value of personal estate £170-7s-5d.[1]

Sister Mary-Ann Severn died shortly afterwards in 1901 and she also directed all her personal estate to go to her brother Charles but, in case he should die before her, she directed everything was to go to William Harvey Whiston, their solicitor. In the event her brother Charles died about the same time as Mary-Ann and her estate went to the solicitor.

Charles Severn 1831-1900

Youngest son Charles did not marry and the 1861 census shows him residing with his spinster Aunt Anne, or rather she was residing with him.

Charles was stated to be a farmer of 200 acres which perhaps suggests he inherited from both his father (who had 53 acres) and his uncle Jonathan (who had 154). As mentioned it is difficult to explain why his older brother did not get this inheritance, unless his brother William

---

[1]   DRO: Will of William Severn 1891, I.D. 727

was already in receipt of an inheritance from his other Uncle Charles.

By the next census in 1871, the number of acres he farmed had been revised down to 189 acres at Elvaston. Sister Jane was living with him at this time and he had the assistance of two labouring boys and his residence was Borrowash Lane. Three years later the following article appears in the Derby Mercury of 22nd July 1874 concerning him.

ALLEGED HORSE STEALING

Joseph Burn, a platelayer of Elvaston was charged with stealing a mare. Property of Charles Severn, farmer of Elvaston. Charles went to see the horse only to find Joseph sat on it heading to the turnpike. Charles seized him, conveyed him to his house where he was kept in the kitchen till the village policeman arrived. Charles and his men had been late up that evening making hay.

The April census of 1891 shows Charles living with his sister Mary Anne (who died ten years later) and both were single. A few weeks later in May, Kelly's Directory of Derby, Notts, Leics & Rutland pp203-4 shows the chief land owners of Elvaston as being, besides the Earl of Harrington, Messrs Charles Severn and John Beggs.[1]

---

[1]   Other records include: burial of Ann Severn on 25 March 1835, age 73 years, at Elvaston. Also TNA: IR 26/355/622 Abstract Will of William Severn,

Charles's brother William had died by this time and Charles perhaps inherited his acres. Charles died in 1900 and was buried at Elvaston Churchyard.

In his Will Charles left his personal estate to sister Mary Ann and his real estate was to be divided between his sister and William Harvey Whiston, the solicitor, and Richard Finney, farmer of Hemington, upon trust to sell everything and invest the money in public stocks to supply an income for Mary Ann for her life. After her death, funds were to be dispersed to; friend George Russell of Sandiacre, Veterinary Surgeon £200, Emma and Annie Russell, daughters of George Russell £100 each, Charles Jordan of Elvaston and Emma his wife £100. Thomas Henry Ashby of Alvaston, Surgeon, £100. Sarah Thompson of Ashby-de-la-Zouch £100. Emma Smith, wife of Arthur (labourer) £50, Robert Harrison of Elvaston 'now living with me' £50. Gilbert Murray of Orchard Dale, Girvan, Ayr £100. John Briggs of Chellaston, licensed victualler £100. William Harvey Whiston, solicitor, £200. Residue of estate to Edward Finney, auctioneer, son of Richard Finney.

Gentleman, of Elvaston (proved at Lichfield) 15th Oct 1805

EMMA SEVERN 1825-1904

Emma, the second daughter of William and Elizabeth Severn married Charles Allsop on 6th October 1855 at Elvaston Church. He was a farmer of Postern Valley in Duffield. And died aged 51 years of age in 1874. The couple had no children and, after his death, Emma returned to Elvaston to reside with her siblings.[1]

- o - o - o -

Thus ended the line of Severns with their long association with Elvaston and the Stanhope family. The lines of descent failed due to a preponderance of unmarried relations or, where there was a marriage, no children from the marriages. William Severn's Will saw the dissipation of the Severn family's wealth amongst a range of friends and the Severn name disappears, as farmers at least on Stanhope lands, in Elvaston.

---

[1]   Marriage Allegation of Charles Allsop of Postern, Duffield, bachelor and Emma Severn.

WILLIAM STANHOPE, 1719-79, 2nd Earl of Harrington

William was known as Viscount Petersham until he succeeded to the Harrington Earldom in 1756 after his father's death. William was the eldest of twins and his mother died at, or just after, the birth. His father's career demanded his presence abroad for most of the time leaving William and his brother Thomas precious little family life.

After attending Eton, William joined the army as in Ensign and saw active service during the War of Austrian Succession. He advanced through the ranks in the army, becoming Colonel of 2nd Troop of Horse Grenadier Guards and then Captain of the 1st Regiment of Foot Guards, whilst at the same time holding a seat in Parliament as Whig MP for Aylesbury 1741-47. He had been present at the Battle of Fontenoy where he had sustained a slight injury.

He made a minimal impact in Parliament but achieved some level of infamy for his own, and his wife's, lifestyles. In 1746 he married the 24 year old Lady Caroline Fitzroy, eldest daughter of the 2nd Duke of Grafton[1] who had been the Lord Chamberlain and the

---

[1]   In 1732 the 10 year old Caroline had captivated the heart of Lord Hervey who described her as "the best bred woman, the most agreeable dancer, the

couple had numerous children.[1]

It is perhaps likely that William and Caroline met in Ireland as William accompanied his father to Dublin when he was appointed Lord Lieutenant-General and Governor General of Ireland. Caroline played hostess for the Lord Lieutenant's Ball at Dublin Castle in 1750 after their marriage. It was at this ball that two teenage sisters, the Gunnings, managed to get invites and attended wearing costumes loaned to them from the Dublin theatre. Making use of their new connection with Caroline and the Harringtons, they followed them back to London where a presentation at court was managed as William had placed the girls in the house of the Duchess of Bedford, so the Harringtons played a key role in facilitating the social mountain climb of the two young girls. The beauty of the young girls took London by storm and, within a short period of time, one Gunning sister became the Duchess of Hamilton and the other became the Countess of Coventry.[2] After being widowed, Elizabeth Gunning, one time Duchess of Hamilton became the Duchess of Argyll.

William's wife Caroline was known as one of the

---

genteelest and the prettiest creature that ever lived". Letters to and from Henrietta, Countess of Suffolk and Her Second Husband … by George Berkeley

[1]   It was said that neither he, nor his father, had a single foot of land to make any settlement with

[2]   Maria's unfortunate habit of using mercury-based make-up led to her premature death at just 27 years of age

"Beauty Fitzroys", a great beauty who had an extraordinary capacity for conversation but whose manners and morals were considered lax. It was also reported that she had liaisons with both men and women during her marriage. George Augustus Selwyn, a somewhat eccentric satirist, unkindly commented on seeing her one day, "Look, there's my Lady Euston and my lady us'd to 't!"[1]

She was a popular character and her high spirits were, on occasion, too much even for her husband. Horace Walpole recounted, in a letter to Mr Montagu, receiving an invitation in 1750 from Lady Caroline to join a party on a visit to Vauxhall pleasure gardens. He wrote *"I had a card from Lady Caroline Petersham, to go with her to Vauxhall. I went accordingly to her house ... We issued into the Mall to assemble our company, which was all the town, if we could get it; for just so many had been summoned"*.[2]

At this point, Walpole describes how the gathered crowd were joined by Lord Petersham *"with his hose and legs twisted to every point of crossness"* and described how he sullenly rode up and down the company and refused to acknowledge his wife when she

---

[1]   Walpole Letters, Vol. 3, p115

[2]   Chronicles of Fashion: From the Time of Elizabeth to the Early Part of the Nineteenth Century, in Manners, Amusements, Banquets, Costumes. Vol. 2 by Elizabeth Stone, 2011

called to him. Caroline approached her husband directly and asked *"Do you go with us, or are you going anywhere else?"* The tort reply she got was *"I don't go with you, I am going somewhere else"* and left Caroline without speaking to anyone else.

Walpole described the merriment of the party; some drunkenness, a comment which almost led to a duel, a new bride being abandoned and the whole party garnering widespread attention in their amusement. Caroline's vivacity was in marked contrast to her husband's and it is often reported that her behaviour was licentious.

As well as Walpole's description of him as being Peter Shambles,[1] society more widely knew him as the "goat of quality" due to his visits, four times a week, to Sarah Prendergast's brothel in King's Place, St James. This particular brothel was also used by Caroline who used to meet there with a group of female friends, their association was called the "New Female Coterie" where like-minded ladies (referred to as demimondaines) congregated and confederated together. Caroline had actually been blackballed by the original founders of this group. One of those who joined this group was Seymour Fleming, who spent a lot of time with Caroline - Seymour being the sister of Caroline's daughter-in-law Jane

---

[1]   Letters from the Hon. Horace Walpole to George Montagu, 23rd June 1750

Fleming. Seymour had been involved in a high profile scandal involving her husband Lord Worsley who brought a criminal conversation case for £20,000 against her.

Caroline went to Paris in 1752 though it is not known if her husband went with her, she was in company with Lady Coventry, another renowned beauty, though Horace Walpole reports, after they returned to England, it was reported that Lady Petersham was not considered handsome and neither was Coventry.

There are a great many mentions of Caroline in the correspondence of Horace Walpole and the Stanhopes must have been residing in close proximity to Walpole's Strawberry Hill residence. For example, on 29th June 1754 Walpole wrote again to George Montagu that he had no news for him as there were so few people in town, but mentioned that Lady Caroline Petersham "had scraped together a few foreigners, after her christening; but I cannot say that the party was much livelier than if it had met at Madam Montandre's".[1] The christening referred to here was the birth of William and Caroline's son Henry in 1754. By the 1750s Stanhope's army career saw him promoted to Major-General and then in

____

[1] Letters from the Hon. Horace Walpole to George Montagu, 1754. Madam Montandre was the widow of Francis de la Rochefaucauld, Marquis of Montandre

1756 his father died and he inherited the earldom and estates.

In 1765 William attended the funeral of the Duke of Cumberland, the third and youngest son of King George II. The ceremony took place at Henry 7th Chapel at Westminster Abbey in the royal vault. Harrington was one of the train of people walking behind the hearse which was drawn by six white horses adorned with white feathers. There were the sounds of drums, trumpets and guns were fired in salute and church bells were rung throughout London and Westminster. The Clarenceux, King of Arms carried a coronet on a black, velvet cushion and 14 yeomen of the guard carried the coffin. Alongside Harrington, there was his father-in-law, the Duke of Grafton who was the chief mourner. Artillery guns were fired in the nearby parks.

The Stanhopes were, of course, present at the coronation of King George III in 1760 where Walpole describes rather cruelly "My Lady Harrington, covered with all the diamonds she could borrow, hire or seize and with the air of Roxana, was the finest figure at a distance ...." (Roxana being wife of Alexander the Great).

Another incident concerning Caroline was told, again by Walpole, which illustrates perhaps the indiscretion of Caroline: "Your friend Lady C___ P _____, [Caroline Petersham] not to let the town quite lapse into politics, has entertained it with a new scene. She was t'other night at the play with her court; viz. Miss Ashe, Lord Barnard, Mons St. Simon, and her favourite footman Richard (whom, under pretence of keeping places, she always keeps in her box, the whole time, to see the play at his ease). Mr Stanley, Colonel Vernon and Mr Vaughan, arrived at the very end of the farce, and could find no room but a row and a half in Lady C____'s box. Richard denied their entrance very impertinently: Mr Stanley took him by the hair of his head, dragged him into the passage and thrashed him. The heroine was outrageous - the heroes not at all so. She sent Richard to Fielding for a warrant: he would not grant it; and so it ended".[1]

Her names crops up in 1768 in correspondence between Mrs Delany (Mary Granville) and a Miss Dewes where it was said that Caroline had a quarrel with her daughter Bell (Isabella later married Charles William, Earl of Sefton). Mother and daughter had a difference of opinion over a gentleman which led Mrs Delany to say of the Stanhope ladies, "how despicable a figure those people make in the world, who have given their whole life up to vanity and folly".[2]

---

[1]   Letters: With a Memoir and Illustrative Notes by Mary Hervey
[2]   Autobiography and correspondence of Mary Granville, Mrs Delany: volume 4 by Mary Delany, Edited by Augusta Hall, 1862

It was probably in her later years that Caroline befriended Seymour Fleming and in 1771 Lady Harrington, the Duchess of Northumberland and some other ladies helped took the unusual step of setting up an opera (without a license) for a single season in 1771 at Mrs Cornely's (a.k.a 'The Empress of Pleasure') rooms in Soho Square.[1] Caroline Duchess of Harrington, the Duchess of Northumberland Elizabeth Percy and Elizabeth Chudleigh Duchess of Kingston were all patrons of Mrs Cornelys and her glittering, celebrity laden and scandalous socials.

William continued his life of debauchery right to the end. Also nicknamed "Lord Fumble," it is doubtful he spent much time at Elvaston Castle as his frequent brothel attendances in London would have made that difficult. Other publications were more scathing of him: the Westminster Magazine referred to him as "a person of the most exceptional immorality" and Town & Country magazine claimed he was as "lecherous as a monkey". There is a long list of his lovers, which included a "negress in a feather'd turban".[2]

Not long before his death, there was perhaps the

---

[1]   Fashionable Acts, Opera and Elite Culture in London 1780-1880 by Jennifer Hall-Witt

[2]   Madams, Bands & Brothel Keepers of London by Fergus Linnare. Sarah Prendergast's Brothel was at King's Place, St James, London. Stanhope was also thought to be a member of the Hellfire Club

most salacious scandal of all when, in 1778, he was involved in a brothel scandal. To cater for Stanhope's desire for variety, Sarah Prendergast sent out to loan two whores from a neighbouring brothel. The ladies gave Stanhope his "pleasure", but were unhappy at only receiving three shillings in exchange. He was, after all an earl. They were Elizabeth Cummings (Country Bet) and Black Susan. Both, when confronted by brothel owner Mrs Butler, refused to give her cut of the money when she demanded it and so Mrs Butler seized their clothes in lieu. The matter was brought to court by the women and, during depositions, it was said that Stanhope visited Sarah Prendergast's brothel on Mondays, Wednesdays, Fridays and Sundays, having two girls each time.

When the story was published in the newspapers Stanhope was furious and he instructed that all newspapers be bought up, to prevent the story getting out. Then, so as not to damage the brothel industry, a bizarre ball was held where masked naked people danced in order to raise money. Stanhope was a contributor.

- o - o - o -

William Stanhope's younger twin brother Thomas likewise joined the army and, in August 1741, had a commission in Captain Honeywood's Regiment of

Dragoons.   He died overseas still in army service, unmarried and childless.

- o - o - o -

When it came to his son's marriage, William stalled matters by quibbling over the marriage settlement figure which resulted in the marriage being postponed for a period of two years.   Clearly William's finances were not in good shape despite the inheritances he received in later life and he died on 1st April 1779.

Daughter Isabella[1] married Richard Molyneux and became 1st Countess of Sefton.

---

[1]   The Harrington name prevails today in Toxteth, Liverpool in honour of Isabella through a scheme for laying out streets by her husband the Earl of Sefton

The second Earl of Harrington's daughter Anna Maria married twice. Her first husband was Thomas Pelham Clinton, 3rd Duke of Newcastle, who died in 1795. Five years later Anna Maria married Charles Gregan Craufurd 1763-1821. The above brass plate, however, is displayed in a prominent position in the central aisle of Elvaston Church, showing Craufurd deaths prior to Anna Maria's marriage into this family. The reason for that was that the vicar of St Bartholomew's in Elvaston was Rev. John Craufurd[1] - in post from 1788 - 1803. The above brass plate shows the vicar's mother Jane and sister Maria who were buried in the church. So the earl's daughter married the vicar's brother.

Area of St Bartholomew's Church where the Harrington family were seated.

---

[1] theclergydatabase.org.uk has the record listed as spelling Crauford

CHARLES STANHOPE, 1753-1829, 3rd Earl of Harrington

Charles is frequently confused with a cousin of the same name. Both were born at the same time, both were Stanhopes, both attended Eton and both were MPs. The following brief details show why:

Charles Stanhope 1753-1829 3rd Earl of Harrington Viscount Petersham	Charles Stanhope 1753-1816 3rd Earl Stanhope Viscount Mahon
1753 Born	1753 Born
1760s Attended Eton	1761 Attended Eton
1769 Army	1764 University of Geneva
1774 MP for Thetford	1774 Failed to obtain seat as MP for Westminster
1776 MP for Westminster	1780 MP for Chipping Wycombe
1777 Engaged to wealthy Heiress Jane Fleming	1774 Married Lady Hester Pitt, dau. of William Pitt the Elder
1779 On father's death, became 3rd Earl of Harrington	1786 On father's death, became 3rd Earl Stanhope
1779 Married Jane Fleming	*Interests: Science (Fellow of the Royal Society)*
Interests: Army/public service	1790 Chairman of the Revolution Society (sympathetic to the aims of the French Revolution)
1798 Privy Councillor	
1805 Ambassador, Vienna	
1806 Ambassador, Berlin	
1806 Privy Councillor, Ireland	
1812 Constable, Windsor Castle	
1829 Died at Brighton	1816 Died at family seat, Chevening, Kent

There was, however, a considerable contrast in political leanings between the two men with the 3rd Earl Stanhope's republican sympathies in sharp contrast to 3rd Earl Harrington's Tory leanings, or rather his tendency to vote with whoever held power at the time. Harrington was not known to speak in the Houses of Parliament whereas Stanhope recorded some 90 speeches and was involved in many inquiries.

Charles (later 3rd Earl of Harrington) was born on 20th March 1753, to William 2nd Earl and Lady Caroline Fitzroy (daughter of the 2nd Duke of Grafton). By the age of 3, when his grandfather died, he became known as Lord Petersham. Charles was a soldier and entered the army as a 16 year old Ensign in the Coldstream Guards. Within a few short years he had the rank of Lieutenant and command of the 29th Foot. In 1774 Charles was on Salisbury Plain for regimental practice when the King inspected the troops there.

Later in that same year Charles became MP for Thetford in a short-lived parliament. Two years later Charles obtained a seat for Westminster which he retained until his was required to relinquish it at his father's death in 1779 when he was raised to the Lords.

In 1776 Charles transferred to the grenadier company of the 29th and, whilst still in his twenties, became aide-de-camp to General Burgoyne, Commander of the British Forces in the North, and was present in service with him on the Saratoga Campaign in Quebec, Canada during the American Revolutionary War where Charles sustained a slight injury. He had fought the Americans at Trois Revières in July 1776 and had also taken part in the failed Hudson Valley Campaign of the following year which was a pivotal moment in the American Revolutionary War. In attempting an unsuccessful manoeuvre with his regiment in Pennsylvania, under the leadership of Sir William Howe, he was forced to surrender his men.[1] Stanhope was sent back to England via New York with Burgoyne's dispatches.

He returned to England in 1777 and, soon after, his engagement was announced to a wealthy heiress called Jane Fleming, daughter and co-heiress of Sir John Fleming of Brompton Park in Middlesex. Any plans to organise a wedding, however, were deferred when his father haggled over the terms of a marriage settlement to such a point that the wedding was delayed. In the mean time Stanhope was busy organising a Regiment of Foot, mustered in the Derby and Nottingham area, near his home at Elvaston Castle. Now the French had joined in the fighting on the American side, it was evident they were planning an attack on the West Indies colonies and Stanhope wanted to raise a regiment (the 85th) and meet the challenge.

At this time his father's health declined and, in April 1779, he died and Charles inherited the title and estate,

---

[1]   A View of the Present State of Derbyshire: with an account of its most remarkable antiquities, by James Pilkington, 1789

becoming 3rd Earl of Harrington. In a matter of weeks after his father's death in April, Charles married Jane Fleming on 23rd May of the same year. Her great fortune was used immediately to clear the Stanhope family's debts and also funds were used by Charles to raise the 85th infantry. After the birth of their son Charles the following year, both Charles and his wife Jane departed for Jamaica with the regiment to defend the island against a possible French invasion. His regiment departed for Jamaica on 30th August 1780 and Stanhope was made a Brigadier-General but his health, like many of those in his regiment, suffered in the environment and he returned to England. The King received him and nominated him in November 1782 as one of his aides-de-camp and conferred the rank of Colonel on him.

Following the death of Lieutenant General Calcraft, Charles was appointed Colonel of the 65th Foot (from 12th March 1783) which departed for Ireland. When the 65th was ordered to America two years later, Stanhope requested permission to return to England where he was given another appointment as Colonel of the 29th Regiment based at Windsor. More honours followed when Stanhope was appointed Colonel of the 1st Regiment of Life Guards with the Gold Stick.

Wife Jane and her sister Seymour were heiresses and

received very large legacies when their father died in 1763. Whilst Seymour, as previously mentioned, had gained notoriety in a scandalous law suit with her husband, Jane's character was seen as the antithesis of her sister, being a model of respectability and virtue. Jane was artistic, Lady of the Bedchamber to Queen Charlotte and a supreme society hostess. She was also a keen amateur painter and friend of Joshua Reynolds and Georgiana Cavendish, Duchess of Devonshire.

When not in town, Charles Stanhope was at Elvaston overseeing the vast Stanhope family's estates in that area within which were two rivers, the Derwent and the Trent and both were prone to flooding and so large areas of land had been given over as flood plains. One place in particular was problematic, being the road from Derby to Nottingham as it enters Sawley. Present-day Sawley Marina is the location (B6540, formerly the A53) and still, in the 21st Century, is subject to occasional flooding despite expensive preventive works. When the road came under water and impassable, there was a long journey of several miles to reach the other side. In the 1780s, previous timber bridges had decayed and ferries and a ford by 1792 were useless due to higher water levels. One of the first things Charles did, within a few years of inheriting the title to the estate, was to set about the construction of 'Harrington Bridge' at this location. Begun in 1786, it was not complete until 1790;

as it took two attempts after the first construction was washed away by the Trent in flood.

Harrington's motives may not have been entirely altruistic since the bridge, when completed, was subject to toll charges, with only Harrington himself and locals in the immediate area being exempt. The bridge still survives, being some 90 metres in length spanning six stone arches. The original toll booth is long gone and wear and tear had meant the middle section has been replaced but the outer arches still survive.[1]

The Earl had plans to redevelop Elvaston Castle[2] and the couple divided their time between there and Harrington House, [3] their London home in Whitehall Gardens. They indulged in lavish entertainment when in London when the cream of society would be in attendance, including George III. Jane "would go out in the morning and pay about thirty calls, leaving at each house an invitation bidding her friends to assemble at Harrington House that same evening".[4] Her Stanhope

---

[1]   Historic Listed Building Structure: Co-ordinates 52.8754 deg N 1.3012 deg W

[2]   Most of the present structure of Elvaston Castle dates from 1815. Capability Brown had earlier declined the commission to landscape the grounds fearing they were too flat and featureless. The death of the original architect, James Wyatt, led to the redevelopment of Elvaston being passed to Robert Walker who worked to Wyatt's design

[3]   Tax records for 1798 show Harrington House next to Carlton House, with the Duke of Marlborough and Lord Godolphin as neighbours. Residence: St Martin in the Fields, Midx. Vol.7, 1798-99

relations at 28 Grosvenor Square (her husband's cousins) were frequently in attendance at her gatherings which took place three or four times a week.

These frequent ensembles in the fashionable habit, encouraged by Jane, of serving the expensive beverage of tea at every opportunity led to the comment that 'if you saw a Stanhope, there you saw a tea-pot'. Indeed, it was Anna-Maria Stanhope, daughter of Charles and Jane who, as she later became Duchess of Bedford, was attributed with making afternoon tea fashionable (the beverage accompanied by a piece of cake being more usual).

From 1788 onwards there were frequent mentions of Charles and his engagements connected with the royal circle and attendance at various levées. Charles had been transferred on 28th January 1788 from the 65th Foot to the 29th Regiment and on 7th February following the death of Lieutenant-General Tryon, The Times carried the following notice:- "Yesterday the Earl of Harrington kissed his Majesty's hand upon his appointment to the command of the 29th Regiment of Foot."

It had been considered, as early as April 1788, to give Harrington the rank of Ambassador to Russia,[1] as cited in

---

4   The Letter-Bag of Lady Elizabeth Spencer-Stanhope, Vol I, by A.M.W. Stirling (Compiled from the Cannon Hall Papers 1806-73)

The Times on 17th April of that year, when notice of a Dutch Treaty was posted and it was said "The Earl of Harrington does not replace Mr Fitzherbert at Petersburg as was intended. His terms of going to that Court were that he should have the rank of Ambassador, which the King did not think proper to comply with; in consequence of which his Lordship has declined going". So clearly the King was hesitant to appoint Harrington the rank that he desired, preferring him instead to remain with the 29th.

In October 1789 Harrington, who was at his country residence in Elvaston, wrote to Lord Cathcart[1] in which he described having just returned from Tynemouth where the regiment had been based and described their route march south. He told Cathcart that he and Lady Harrington had taken a day out to visit Lord Darlington as they passed near his residence before catching up with the regimental march at North Allerton. He discussed with Cathcart arrangements for when the regiment would arrive in London en route to Chatham.

On 16th November 1789, Lord and Lady Harrington arrived at Dartford and they had their 5 year old son Leicester with them. After meeting up with Cathcart the

---

[1]   BL, Add MS 28063, fols 122, 146
[1]   Grandson of Charles Lord Cathcart who commanded an expedition to America in 1740 and died en route

whole party made their way to Rochester and then on to Dover. Writing to his wife, Cathcart commented on the Harringtons *"I marched most of the way from Dartford, and I am very hungry, but I shall go early and drink tea with Lady Harrington where several of our officers are to be. I have not seen such a military world a great while. Lord H [Harrington] is delighted and is strutting about the parade with Crosby, viewing a parcel of ragamuffins of different corps who are being tormented in different corners by a variety of drill serjeants."*[1]

On the following day, 17th November, when the regiment was to depart Dover, Cathcart wrote again to his wife who was in confinement waiting the birth of a child. He described dining with the Harringtons where, of course, there was plenty of tea drinking but how he had left a supper Lady Harrington had arranged in her apartments as he was tired. The Harringtons' departure from London was noted in the court circular: *"On Sunday evening the Earl and Countess of Harrington set off from their house in Stable Yard, St James's for Dover."*

By 20th November, Harrington and Cathcart arrived at Dover Castle where the regiment was based and Lord Harrington was said to be suffering a *"slight fit of the*

---

[1]   History of the 29th (Worcestershire) Regiment by H. Everard, Chapter 6, 1788-1789

gout". Two days later Cathcart told his wife *"Poor Lord H is unable to walk; no pain, but weakness and swelling and is forced to hop about his room with the help of the walls"*. The accommodation was described as bare and stark by Cathcart but Lord and Lady Harrington had arranged for their own furniture to arrive at their Dover lodgings by sea and so were immensely comfortable. There were further reports by Cathcart of Harrington's gout problems, he said *"Lord H has his leg on a stool and has had three relapses, and has suffered much pain; they will return to town as soon as he is able"*.[1]

An interesting minor detail to emerge from Cathcart's letters was the presence of a Frenchman in the ranks who was a master draftsman and Lady Harrington, with an interest in art and painting, had been having lessons in perspective from him. By 17th December, Cathcart told his wife that Harrington's foot and ankle were so badly swollen that he could put no weight on them. Three days later, on 20th December, the Harringtons were making preparations to leave Dover Castle after a meal of venison, which apparently was well to their liking. It seems likely that the Harringtons were going to stay with Mrs Cathcart after leaving Dover as Cathcart told his wife "you will like her because she really wishes to be agreeable and civil, I do not recollect to have heard

---

[1]   History of the 29th (Worcestershire) Regiment by H. Everard, Chapter 6, 1788-1789

her abuse anybody, or say anything ill-natured or satirical".

Before they left, however, Lord and Lady Harrington left a Christmas bonus for the soldiers left at the barracks. Lord Harrington left a guinea for each company of men and Lady Harrington donated a brown flannel great coat to every soldier's child in the regiment, the coats had been made in the same manner as her own children wore. Cathcart said "you cannot imagine how comfortable and creditable it makes the little things look".[1]

On 23rd December 1791, as reported in The Times, Harrington once more sought a noble position but was overlooked, as it was reported *"Last night the Duchess of Gordon arrived in town from Scotland. Princess Sophia of Gloucester was not present at the Duchess of Cumberland's route: It was His Majesty's wish to have given the rangership of the park (Windsor) to Lord Harrington who really is in want of such a noble provision, but Lord Grenville's interest preponderated, and so he was made Ranger for life"*.

So Harrington contented himself, again, with the movements of his regiment, now 1st Life Guards: 23rd Oct 1792 - The Times, London, "On Sunday Lord

---

[1]   History of the 29th (Worc.) Regiment by H. Everard, Chapter 6, 1788-1789

Harrington's regiment marched into Windsor where they are to be quartered during the winter."[1] He would continue to hold his position as Colonel of the 1st Life Guards until his death. Three days later Harrington was in attendance at the King's anniversary at his accession where guns were fired in St James's Park and the Tower. Harrington attended the drawing room of St James's Palace where the Queen held a small gathering.

Stanhope's request in 1793 for his regiment to serve under the Duke of York in Flanders was denied due to his household position, though he received the brevet of Major-General. The King had different ideas for Stanhope and sent him on a private mission to the Duke of York.

On 1st January 1798 he was given the brevet of Lieutenant General and was second in command of the London staff.

By 1798 Harrington had been appointed to the Privy Council and his military accolades continued. Lord Harrington was reported, on 7th August 1802, as arriving at Brighton with the Prince for the Lewes Races in company with the Neapolitan Ambassador Prince Castelcicala where there was much betting. A few years later, on 10th November 1801, Harrington was present[2]

---

[1]   List of General Officers and Colonels of the British Army for 1st February 1793: Colonels: Charles Stanhope 3rd Earl of Harrington

for the Lord Mayor's Day when a new incumbent was sworn into post. The event was enhanced by a variety of street entertainers, musicians, a variety of men in livery and all manner of finely dressed officials and nobles.

In later years Charles Stanhope obtained the coveted role of Ambassador he had sought formerly when he became Ambassador to Vienna (Extraordinary Mission) though Sir Arthur Paget was overall Ambassador in 1805 and then to Berlin after Lord Harrowby. The decision to appoint him as an Ambassador was not a straight forward one and there had been disagreement amongst ministers that Stanhope was not of sufficiently high enough social standing to impress the receiving court. Harrington was well aware of the distinction of rank and, commenting on another's appointment, he said 'In the situation we at present stand with your court, the King did not think fit to appoint a minister of a higher rank'.[1] He had also been appointed Commander-in-Chief of the Forces in Ireland for the period 1805-12 and Privy Councillor of Ireland from 1806 and Constable of Windsor Castle 1812-29. He was subsequently honoured by being awarded GCH, Knight Grand Cross of the Hanoverian order of chivalry in 1821 in recognition of his service and, during the coronation of George IV that year, was the bearer of the Great Standard of

---

[2]   Reported in The Times, London, 10th November 1801
[1]   British Diplomats and Diplomacy, 1688-1800 by Jeremy Black

England.

It was reported in the Morning Post that on 20th October 1823 the King (George IV) had a small gathering at Windsor Castle which included the Earl and Countess Harrington and a few others. The Band of the Royal Horse Guards attended and played sacred music for them.

He died on 11th September 1829 at Brighton and his body was taken to the Stanhope family's London home where those intending to attend his funeral gathered. The cortege, which left at 11am in the morning, included Viscount Petersham, now 4th Earl of Harrington, Leicester Stanhope and Rev Stanhope. It left Stable Yard at St James and the family's state carriage, pulled by four horses, began the long journey back to Elvaston where the funeral would take place the next day. Two other carriages followed the family's state carriage. The coffin was covered in crimson velvet, decorated with coronets and richly ornamented with gilt. Armorial bearings of the Stanhope noble family were on it.[1]

There is a monument at St Bartholomew's Church at his country seat of Elvaston. "To Charles, 3rd Earl of Harrington who died 11th September 1829, aged 76 years."[2] The effigy represents grief and was erected by

---

[1] Leicester Journal, 2nd October 1829

[2] History, Gazetteer and Directory of Derbyshire, with the town of Burton-

his children in 1833. From his career as a professional soldier, Charles's legacy, in practical terms, was twofold: he introduced a newly designed sword that, meeting with royal approval, became standard issue. Secondly, he was an advocate of the military manoeuvres and tactics of David Dundas (who published Principles of Military Movements of 1788) and Stanhope adopted the same model and it became adopted into use.

Elvasto[...]gers, dated 1831, published by Jones & Co. Temple of the Muses, Finsbury Square, London. From a plate reproduced from Jones' 'Views of the Seats of Noblemen and Gentlemen in England, Wales, Scotland and Ireland'

The above image of Elvaston Hall/Castle is an engraved print of 1831 and shows the south side of the house. To the left, just out of frame is the Church of St Bartholomew's and on the far right is the wing of an earlier structure which has the date 1633 on a lintel.

---

upon 1857 by Samuel Bagshaw (of Sheffield)

The garden in the foreground looks bare and in stark contrast to anyone familiar with the elaborate remodelling carried out by the 3rd Earl's son.

The magnificent 'golden gates' seen above were brought by the 3rd Earl to Elvaston from Versailles - the central taller gates only that is, not the wide expanse of railings. After Napoleon's downfall in 1819 the Earl had the gates shipped to Elvaston. They were originally thought to have been situated on a Royal Palace in Madrid before Napoleon acquired them. The gates were originally located much closer to the house, being placed just over 100 yards in front of the south side of the house (where the present parterre garden is). It was the 4th Earl's gardener William Barron who relocated them much further away, to their present location, to make way for enclosing and enlarging the gardens within. They were then flanked by specially made 15 foot high railings made of Birmingham cast iron. Despite the name 'golden', which probably indicates they were originally gilded, the gates were painted the present colour of blue not long after their installation at Elvaston.

The Harrington coat of arms is position on both ends of both columns on the central gate within which, on one at least, a bell can still be seen - to alert the neighbouring lodge (now gone) that there was a visitor.

Either end of the 115ft long gates there are alabaster statues on top of large granite blocks, the one above depicting Hercules and the Nemean Lion (one of the 12 labours of Hercules, the greatest of Greek heroes) the other depicting Jason and the Golden Fleece.

Close up of gate, showing the bell (above)

Harrington coat of arms (below)

It is thought the above memorial to the 3rd Earl of Harrington (in St Batholomew's Church, Elvaston) was by Canova, the most celebrated artist in Europe, but since Antonio Canova died in 1822, some seven years before the memorial dated 1829, then perhaps the sculpture was done prior to the 3rd Earl's death and adapted to become a memorial to his memory from his children afterwards.

Wife Jane, who in 1782 was considered one of the best dressed women at court, alongside Georgiana Duchess of Devonshire, continued her post as Lady of the Bedchamber to Charlotte of Mecklenburg-Stretlitz, wife of George III. Jane died on 3rd February 1824 at St James's Palace and was buried a week later at Westminster Abbey.

CHARLES STANHOPE, 1780-1851, 4th Earl of Harrington

Charles was the eldest son of Charles Stanhope 3rd Earl and was born on 8th April 1780 at his parents' town residence Harrington House in London. He went by the name Viscount Petersham until he inherited the earldom on his father's death in 1829 and it was perhaps inevitable, given the 'beau monde' into which Charles was born, that he would grow up a dandy and a pleasure-seeking man of fashion.

Like his brothers, Charles became acquainted with Harriet Wilson, a celebrated Regency courtier who became the mistress of Lord Craven, the Prince of Wales and Wellington. In fact, her revelations about Wellington led to him coining the phrase 'publish and be damned'. Harriet relates some of her conversations she had with the Stanhope siblings in her memoirs but Charles Lord Petersham in particular. This was one conversation, where Charles said,

"If you are the sort of spirited, independent, fine creature I have always heard you were, you will allow me to accompany you home, immediately as fast as our horses can drive us".

Harriet replied, "Just the sort of thing I like best. If

______" and I paused.

"If what?" said he.

"If I happened to have a fancy for you but, frankly, I have none!"

"Upon your honour and word you do not like me?" Petersham asked, with evident astonishment.

"No, really" said I, "although you are very handsome but you are not my style of man. I am alluding to your foppery ….."

"What is it you dislike about me?" Petersham asked. And so on. She wished him a good morning and left.

He was perceived as somewhat eccentric, with affected mannerisms, an artistic turn and a passion for tea drinking and collecting snuff boxes.

The liking Charles had for tea, inherited from his parents, was also held by his sister Anna Maria. Anna Maria had been Lady of the Bed Chamber to Queen Victoria 1837-41 and married the 7th Duke of Bedford. She is attributed with making afternoon tea fashionable when, lamenting the long hours between lunch and dinner, she congregated fashionable ladies in her rooms for Darjeeling tea and sandwiches/cakes about 5pm in the afternoon, and thus the practice was begun. Anna

Maria was also known for some cruel gossip she instigated about Lady Flora Hastings. Flora was unmarried and Anna Maria began a rumour that she may be pregnant and speculated on the father of the child being Sir John Conroy. Flora, however, was not pregnant and died shortly afterwards from cancer and so Anna Maria was chastised for tarnishing the good lady's reputation.

Charles Stanhope joined the army at an early age after rebelling against the brutal regime of Eton and became an Ensign in the Coldstream Guards at just 15 years of age. He rose through the ranks becoming Captain of the 10th Regiment, Prince of Wales' Own, Light Dragoons and in February 1803 was appointed Major of the Queen's Rangers.

About this time, as his father was about to take up his appointment as Ambassador to Vienna and Berlin, there was a family settlement made concerning Charles who was now of full age:

20th July 1804:
First party: 3rd Earl Harrington
Second party: 4th Earl Harrington
Third parties: Earl of Moira and Lord Mulgrave

This family settlement concerned manors and estates held by the 3rd Earl in the County of Chester which were to be held by the Earl of Moira and Lord Mulgrave upon trust for raising of portions for those children the 4th Earl was expected to have. The family estate at Elvaston was, of course, entailed on the male heirs but the 3rd Earl made provision for any children from Charles 4th Earl, thereby allowing his son, for example, to leave any daughters well provided for. With the passage of time, the Earl of Moira and Lord Mulgrave were replaced as trustees of the Indenture of Settlement by the Dukes of Bedford and Leinster who later became brothers-in-law of Charles.

Charles subsequently served as Lieutenant Colonel of the 3rd West India Regiment in 1807 though, by 1812, he was languishing on half pay and so accepted an appointment as Lord of the Bedchamber to King George III, an appointment he continued with the accession of George IV (he had been a close friend of the Prince Regent) where he was joined by his cousin Robert Henry Stanhope who was another Groom of the Bedchamber.

It was said that Charles resembled in appearance Henry Quatre of France and he became quite a trend-setter with a range of accoutrements being named after him by those who emulated his style; such as the Petersham overcoat and Petersham ribbon (thick corded material to stiffen hat bands etc). He was also a collector of paraphernalia connected to the tea-making process and he also had a very large collection of snuff boxes and canes.[1] He had, it was said, a snuff box for every single day of the year.

Charles, who supposedly never stirred out of doors before 6pm, still went by the title Viscount Peter-sham when he became smitten by a woman twenty years his junior.

The woman Charles became enamoured with was an actress, and the notion of a future Earl having a relationship with an young actress was a scandal of the first degree.

Her name was Maria Foote and an article, written in 1824-25 about Maria, described her exposure to the world of theatre at 12 years of age and said *"To those*

---

[1]   In 1816, his youngest brother Augustus was brought before a court martial over gambling debts. Whilst in Cambray, France, Lieutenant Stanhope of the 12th Regiment of Light Dragoons, and another, had engaged a very young Lord Beauchamp (barely 16 years of age) in a game of cards, plied him with drink leading to the young Lord being £8,000 in debt to Stanhope and £7,000 in debt to the other player. Officers as Horse Guards took a dim view of this behaviour which they said was "unbecoming the character of an Officer and a Gentleman" and discharged him from His Majesty's service. A Collection of the Charges, Opinions, and Sentences of General Courts .... by Charles James

who know nothing of a theatre, it may be new to tell them, that an interesting girl is in the jaws of ruin who enters it as an actress, unless watched and protected by her family and friends with the scrutiny of Argus, without his disposition to fall asleep. Constantly exposed to the gaze of men, inflaming a hundred heads and agitating a thousand hearts …. Let the reader fancy an innocent girl, from a country town, plunged at once into this furnace of depravity".[1]

The above article was written before Maria married Charles and so, if a Viscount marrying an actress seems a small issue today, it was far more than that at the time. When they did eventually marry, Charles had just become 5th Earl Harrington and Maria became a Countess.

Charles had been fond of attending opera and the theatre and began a relationship with Maria Foote in the late 1820s. Maria was the daughter of Samuel T Foot, a Theatre Manager in Plymouth who had encouraged his young daughter to appear on stage as Juliet (in Romeo and Juliet). Maria had a successful career on stage and appeared in 1814-25 at Covent Garden as Amanthis in 'The Child of Nature' which had been adapted from the French 'Madam de Genlis' by Elizabeth Inchbald and she

---

[1]   The Drama; or Theatrical Pocket Magazine forming a complete critical and biographical illustration of the British Stage, Vol. 1824 to May 1825

later performed in Virginius by Sheridan Knowles.

Maria Foote's previous relationships and stormy private life had gained her enormous notoriety and infamy. She had been the mistress of Colonel William Berkeley, later Earl Fitzhardinge, with whom she had two children. When Berkeley dithered over committing himself to marrying Maria, she moved on to a new relationship with Joseph Hayne of Burdeson Park in Wiltshire and a wedding day was fixed. Maria, on anticipation of entering her new state of marriage, handed over custody of her two children to Berkeley but, when Hayne learned of Maria's past, he took fright. The turmoil of his mind led to a re-arranged marriage, followed by another cancellation and the relationship ended. What Maria did next astonished many as she sued Hayne for breach of promise and demanded £20,000 damages.

What she got was £3,000 damages but enormous public sympathy and, when she returned to the stage after the trial, it was to sell-out audiences at Covent Garden.

After appearing at Drury Lane, she began touring with the theatre company for some five years the length and breadth of Britain, until finally her path crossed with Charles Stanhope.

Maria Foote, later Countess of Harrington

The 3rd Earl of Harrington was still alive at this time and was not impressed by his eldest son's choice of partner. Charles prudently waited until his father's death before bringing Maria back to his seat at Elvaston where the couple married on 7th April 1831.

Charles ceased his employment as Lord of the Bedchamber after marriage as it would have been impossible, for example, for Maria to be presented at court. Charles would have been wounded by the reaction of his friends to Maria and chose this time to retire to his country seat at Elvaston Castle where Maria would not have had to experience being shunned by smart London society.

Elvaston became a secluded retreat for the couple and from this time onwards, Charles devoted enormous energy to transforming the house and its gardens into his vision of a unique, ideal home.

It was very much a retreat and no visitors were invited there, though there is evidence that close family were. One small section of garden to the north in the direction of the lake was designed by his sisters and is called 'Garden of the Three Sisters' and certain avenues through the estate were named after his brothers-in-law.

They certainly did not abandon their London life as Harrington House was retained and Charles would have needed to visit London frequently not least to oversee the management of his extensive estate in South Kensington.

Back in Derbyshire, Lewis Cottingham, a specialist in Gothic revival was the 4th Earl's architect and created a "dream home" for the Earl and Countess though it was following on from the redesign of the house which had been started by the 3rd Earl with his architect James Wyatt who did not live to see the transformation.

Hall of the Fair Star - Elvaston Castle 2016

The impressive entrance hall contained suits of tilting armour from the Elizabethan era, the dining room having a chimney piece bearing the 'arms and quarterings of the family of Stanhope with the crest in an upper compartment'; tapestries hung in the drawing room depicting the story of Don Quixote.[1]

The theme of the 'Fair Star' was a tribute to Maria. Inside the gothic hallway, in the doorway from the hall to the staircase, in the overhead architrave, you can read the words 'Beauty is a Witch' (to be read from the hall side).

---

[1]   The English Counties Delineated, Vol. 2 by Thomas Moule, p164 Midland Circuit, 1837

The above picture was taken from standing in the doorway looking up towards the ceiling and the sentiments were taken from Shakespeare's 'Much Ado About Nothing':[1]

Don John:
Signor, you are very near my brother in his love. He is enamored on Hero. I pray you, dissuade him from her. She is no equal for his birth. You may do the part of an honest man in it.

Claudio:
How do you know he loves her?

Don John:
I heard him swear his affection.

Borachio:
So did I too, and he swore he would marry her tonight.

---

[1]   Much Ado About Nothing. Act 2, Scene 1, 172-178, speech by Claudio

Don John:
Come, let us to the banquet. Exeunt Don John and Borachio

Claudio: (unmasking)
*Friendship is a constant in all other things save in the office
and affairs of love therefore all hearts in love use their own
tongues.*
*Let every eye negotiate for itself and trust no agent, for
beauty is a witch against whose charms faith melteth into
blood.*
This is an accident of hourly proof, which I mistrusted not.
Farewell, therefore, Hero.

Maria Foote had played Beatrice, one of the lovers, in Much Ado About Nothing in 1829.[1]

These words seem so symbolic and appropriate to the 4th Earl and his actress wife who was so well below him in rank. The story of lovers who are deceived into thinking each other false and whose friends try to persuade them against marrying must have resonated with Charles Stanhope. Don John begs Claudio to persuade her brother to change his mind about marrying a woman who is not of his rank as Charles Stanhope, no doubt, faced repeated attempts by friends and relations not to get involved with Maria the actress.

In placing this phrase in such a prominent position in his house Charles seems to be making a loud statement: that all lovers should look to their own hearts, not rely

---

[1]   Much Ado About Nothing by Alison Findlay, 1988

on the persuasions and opinions of others. Charles had spurned unsympathetic friends in favour of the love of his wife and beauty, to him, was a witch's spell that had turned loyalty into passion. He never thought it would happen to him, of course, and the symbolism is that romantic love can break the bond of friendship if that friendship attempts to interpose itself.

It is a bold and very personal statement and the story's inclusion of Hero being jilted at the altar and consequently being despised by her father who wished her dead, was the situation wife Maria had been in before she met Charles. It was symbolic of their relationship and, perhaps poignantly, was the story of love triumphing over adversity.

Maria had appeared in 'Much Ado about Nothing' on 13th March 1829[1] and also performed a dance from 'Cherry and Fair Star' (A Grand Eastern Spectacle) at Bath later that year. All this took place before her marriage to the 4th Earl of Harrington but after their relationship had begun.

The romantic theme was extended into the gardens, including architecture such as the creation of a Moorish temple which contained a statue of the Earl and his wife, with Charles kneeling at Maria's feet.

---

[1]   The Dramatic Magazine, Issue 1, 1829

The garden facing due south of the main entrance to the house was called the Mon Plaisir Garden (later Bower Garden), or Garden of the Fair Star and contained elaborate topiary and gilded statues and the contrast of gold and green was exquisite. It was a busy landscape with an exotic monkey tree as a centrepiece, water features and rock formations which transformed a hitherto plain landscape.

Inspired by 17th century designs, the focal point was an 8-point star-shaped planting with recessed bowers from clipped yews encircling statues. From the central star there were 8 bowers of Cydonia Japonica and walls of yew large arched over at sufficient height to walk inside with light supplied by periodic cut out windows. The parkland was planted with mature trees which the Earl's Scottish gardener William Barron made a speciality skill in contriving novel ways of transporting them from wherever their source was.

From Veitch's 'Manual of the Coniferae' Topiary Work - The Yew Garden at Elvaston Castle 1887. Similar to E. Adveno Brooke's 1857 View of 'Mon Plaisir' in 'The Gardens of England'

The most elaborate of the gardens at Elvaston Castle (south side); The Moorish Temple (which still exists) can be seen top right, took some 80 gardeners to maintain. Every known species of pine tree, usually mature ones, was brought in and a paradise of evergreens, with lake and rock formations was created as a unique pleasure garden solely for the benefit for Charles and Maria.

It was a garden the like of which had never been seen before. It was pure romanticism with gardens designed to look like paintings and so artistic they could inspire poetry and captivate the audience. There was also a pine plantation interspersed with man-made rocky formations, some of which were 50 feet tall, and a lake, which brought a touch of the Alps in summer to the plain, flat fields of Derbyshire. Twenty feet tall marble statues in rich gilt with basins and fountains stunned the senses. The 4th Earl's garden was described, in 1870, as "the most wonderful place in England, and probably the world, for its topiary as well as collections of evergreens".[1]

Charles and Marie had two children, though their son died aged just four and with only a daughter left, the Elvaston estate had to be entailed to a male heir and so, after Charles died, it would pass to his brother. In anticipation of this eventuality, Charles made arrangements to financially secure his wife and daughter in his lifetime and, referring back to the previously mentioned family settlement, he arranged some £5,000 to be available to them after his demise.

---

[1]   From 'Skeleton Tours'

Executors of his will:

Charles Stanhope	Anna-Maria Stanhope	Charlotte-Augusta Stanhope
mar'd Maria Foote	mar'd Francis Russell	mar'd Angus Fitzgerald
actress	7th Duke of Bedford	3rd Duke of Leinster
	Brother was Prime Minister x2	aka Marquess of Kildare
		Charles William Fitzgerald
		4th Duke of Leinster and
		Marquess of Kildare

William Platt a Barrister of the Inner Temple and Edward Charles Eddrupp of Tennyson Place, Euston Square, Mdx all acted as Executors for the 4th Earl's Will to hold in trust the sum of £5,000 which was due to Charles under the terms and resolution of Harrington v Stanhope (of 1844). The Trust was to be invested to provide maintenance for his wife and daughter, who was 12 years old when Charles wrote his Will in 1845.

The same trustees were to ensure that Harrington House, which Charles leased from the Duke of Pembroke, was available for his wife if she wished to continue to use it or to dispose of the same if she did not.

Daughter Lady Jane St. Maur Blanche Stanhope was born in 1833 and married George, 3rd Marquess Conyngham, a soldier and State Steward to the Lord Lieutenant of Ireland. Later in life he became Equerry to Queen Victoria and died in 1882 at the age of 57. Lady Jane lived on to 1907

Charles died at Brighton in 1851 but his body was returned to Elvaston for burial via the family mansion at Whitehall Gardens. The body arrived at Derby Railway Station at 1pm on 12th March 1851 and the procession consisted of a coach drawn by four horses, followed by several carriages and they travelled to Elvaston where the burial took place. Maria arrived at Derby later that day with her daughter Lady Jane St Maur Blanche Stanhope and they were both present for the interment.[1]

In memory of Charles, Maria had a stained glass window (by Warrington) made in 1851. It is situated at the west end of the church tower and depicts the Good Samaritan, feeding and clothing the hungry - see below.

---

[1]   Derby Mercury, 12th March 1851

Stained Glass Window to the Memory of Charles

It is actually quite difficult to see the above beautiful stained glass window now because, since 1905, it has been covered up when a large organ (which is not currently working) was installed.

St Bartholomew's Church, Elvaston

When Maria died some years later, her body was brought from London (Whitehall) to Derby Railway Station and, like her husband's cortege, was escorted to Elvaston in a hearse, drawn by plumed horses. Reverend Highmore conducted the burial service.

The 5th Earl of Harrington and other family members were present with a few friends and she was interred in a vault in the centre aisle of the church. The coffin was carried by eight of the estate's labourers and an outer coffin, because there was more than one, was covered in violet velvet, studded with silver. 'On the lid was a coronet in silver, and a silver plate bore the following inscription: Maria, Countess of Harrington, Died 27th Dec 1867, aged 69 years'.

Above east aspect of Elvaston Castle

Above west aspect of Elvaston Castle

LEICESTER FITZGERALD CHARLES STANHOPE, 1784-1862
5TH Earl of Harrington

For most of his life the 5th Earl of Harrington was known as the Honourable Leicester Stanhope. He was born on 2nd September 1784 in Dublin Barracks as the third son of Charles 3rd Earl and Jane Fleming.   Like other Stanhopes he made the army his career and joined the 1st Regiment of Life Guards as a Cornet on 1st October 1799 and then later became Sub-Lieutenant.   He advanced through the ranks as he moved to the 9th Regiment of Foot and then the 10th Regiment of Light Dragoons (Prince of Wales Own) a Captain (purchased), the same regiment brother Charles had been in.

Harriet Wilson, the previously mentioned celebrated Regency courtier who became mistress to the Prince of Wales, Lord Craven and Wellington described in her memoirs meeting the Stanhopes. She resided at Marine Parade, Brighton.   One night at the theatre, Harriet noticed a man who had been staring at her 'beauty' for quarter of an hour. She said of him, "He was a very fashionable man; but not at all handsome.   I felt convinced from that certain air de famille, that he must be a Stanhope, although I had never met him before. It was neither Lincoln Stanhope, nor Fitzroy, nor that great unlicked cub, who was turned out of his regiment for black legging, or leaguing with blacklegs.[1] These three I had often met. It must be Leicester ..... who was the less handsome than his brothers".   Speaking of him later, Harriet said "I wanted to have another look at Leicester Stanhope ..... he is ugly methinks and yet I prefer him to any of the handsome Stanhopes, for there is something of better feeling, and more expression in his eyes" ..... "I merely preferred his ugliness to his brother's beauty, because he was the only one of the family who ever seemed to admire me, even for an instant". This was probably directed at Charles, Lord Petersham who Harriet knew very well. Leicester came to Harriet's rescue when she inadvertently wandered into a lobby and felt in need of rescue. That lobby, she said, had the worst type of women in it.

Harriet claimed Leicester was in love with her for a few weeks. "Leicester Stanhope wants me to go to Drury Lane to-night and has taken a private box for me" she stated in her memoirs, though clearly she was not in love with him as she said, "what did I care for Leicester Stanhope, or any of his stupid race, beyond the mere past time these attractions might afford, pour le moment. Therefore I invited Amy to join us."

Leicester, apparently, then fell in love with Amy and

---

[1]   An unlicked cub would be an immature youth lacking manners.
Blacklegging, in this sense, could be a reference to cheating at gaming

Harriet said of their relationship "in less than a fortnight, from that evening, Amy and Leicester were to be found ruralizing together at a retired pot-house in Putney or Clapham, or some such place for their honeymoon! I forget which one of them got tired first, but I know one of them was tired in less than a week and Amy returned to town, and her dear variety!"

To return to his military life. In 1807 he was present in Buenos Aires in South America where he was present it came under attack.[1] Writing about this time, Leicester said: "If the *Holy* Alliance should enter into a confederacy in favour of Ferdinand, and attempt the restoration of South America to that monarch, it would be entirely in vain, even if the South Americans be unaided; for what are the forces that the whole could bring against that numerous people, compared to the well-equipped armies of England ..."[2]

The promotion of the Earl of Moira in 1812 to become Governor-General of British India augured well for Leicester's military career. Francis Rawdon-Hastings went by a variety of different titles in his life; Earl of Moira to Marquis of Hastings; the significance to

---

[1]   Hart's Annual Army List, Special Reserve List. Vol. 6

[2]   Greece, in 1823 and 1824: Being a Series of Letters and Other Documents on the Greek Revolution, written during a visit to that country. To which are added Reminiscences of Lord Byron. 1825 by Leicester Stanhope, Earl of Harrington

Leicester lay in the close family ties. His cousins, Earls of Chesterfield, were direct descendants of Catherine Hastings, daughter of Francis Lord Hastings, eldest son of George 4th Earl of Huntingdon.

During his military service in India, Stanhope became chairman of the committee of leading European inhabitants of Madras and in a meeting to form such a committee the following happened. "On the names of the gentlemen proposed for the committee being read, Colonel Stanhope objected to his name being included as he considered himself as part of the Marquis of Hastings' household and he thought the committee ought to be composed of men perfectly independent and that those gentlemen only should be named who were unconnected with government. This objection, however, was unanimously overruled by the meeting and it was resolved that Colonel Stanhope's name should remain.

In his 'Sketch of the history and influence of the press in British India' Stanhope said "the most important maxim of morality and of politics is this ..... Do no wrong!" Much of the experiences Stanhope went through in India left an indelible impression on him. He would devote much of his interests in later life to those issues he'd become exposed to in India, i.e. emphasis on a free press and on education.

Stanhope dramatically wrote "The Marquis of Hastings abolished the Censorship in British India. This perhaps was the noblest, because it was the most extensively useful act recorded on British annals. A death-blow it was to superstition, with her swarm of gods, and to despotism, the growth of thirty centuries. It was the birth of hope to about one twelfth portion of the human race, and to their offspring from generation to generation. A durable monument it was, which will excite the genius and improvement of every age, and remain in Asia a proud record of the strength and virtue of Britain."

Much of the later actions Stanhope attempted in Greece can be traced to these lessons he learned in India.

In 1813 he published a pamphlet called 'The Military Commentator, or thoughts upon the construction of the Military Code of England: contrasted with that of the codes of other nations together with regard to military flogging' where he expressed his disdain for the practice of flogging soldiers and was critical also of the process of military law.

He was appointed Deputy Adjutant-General 1815-17 whilst serving in the East Indies where he transferred to the 47th Regiment of Foot. He was later appointed Deputy Quartermaster-General for the East Indies during the Third Anglo-Maratha War (or Mahratta War) which was bought to establish the East India Company's control over the region.

Leicester was decorated for his service and made CB, Companion of the Bath. Some of Leicester's medals were sold at auction in 2000, including his C.B. medal for a sum of £4,400. The auctioneer's description was: *"an important Mahratta War C.B. group of three awarded to Colonel Leicester Stanhope, 5th Earl of Harrington, decorated by King Otto for his services to Greece where he was a member of Lord Byron's circle of friends. The Most Honourable Order of The Bath (Military) C.B., breast badge in 22 carat gold and enamels, hallmarked London 1816, complete with gold wide swivel-ring suspension and gold ribbon buckle, minor enamel chips; Army of India 1799-1826, 1 clasp Maheidpore (Lt. Col. The Hon., Dep. Qr. Mr Genl.) short hyphen reverse, impressed naming: Greece, Order of the Redeemer, 1st type, King Otto, Commander's neck badge, gold and enamels, the second with minor contact wear and edge bruise, otherwise generally nearly extremely fine and a rare group (3) - Price guide £3,000-£4,000."*

He resigned as Quartermaster in 1821 and subsequently engaged in hostile newspaper exchanges, such as on 15th October 1821 where he corresponded with 'Old Indian' and 'Carnaticus', two Britons writing under pen names on the issue of Brahmin in India. Leicester wrote "one word more …. much has been said against anonymous writers and those too who fight under false colours. I must however say, in defence of the Old Indian and of Carnaticus, that they have acted with a sort of cautious prudence in not affixing their English names to sentiments so foreign to the character of Britons". The tone of Stanhope's newspaper correspondence was extremely pompous and self-important - traits which emerge from other correspondence of his to be discussed later.

Stanhope also wrote 'Sketch of the History and Influence of the Press in British India' towards the end of his military service in India. He was also opinionated on other matters too. As time went on he became more and more critical of the methods and practices of the East India Company. He also took an active role in the freedom of the press in India - this again was a forerunner to similar campaigns he would run when he moved to Greece.

Like many Europeans who had enjoyed a classical education and become familiar with the world of Ancient Greece, the plight of Greece in the early 1820s prompted him to feel he should become involved in its struggles. So in 1823 he volunteered to serve in Greece as Agent to the London Greek Committee which had been established to support the Greek movement for independence from the Ottoman Empire. Stanhope's particular mission was to influence the development of Greece follow its successful war of independence. Other Europeans, such as Lord Byron, similarly felt sympathetic to the cause and travelled to the country to be part of it.

Stanhope wanted to be part of the formulation of a new Greek constitution, though it turned out that his particular vision did not entirely coincide with what the Greek's themselves wanted.

Leicester was a very close friend, and admirer, of Jeremy Bentham - the founder of modern utilitarianism and Stanhope drew heavily on Bentham's ideas in his attempt to draft out a constitution. Bentham was very keen to help Stanhope because he felt that Greece, in particular, was a country with the potential to bring about an idyllic new constitution, having none of the hindrances that many other nations did. They had thrown off the yoke of the Muslim Ottoman empire, they had no colonies, no king, no nobility and, as he wrote to the legislators of Greece in 1823, "your minds are not under the tyranny of lawyers".[1]

Leicester worked alongside those who would become

---

[1]   J. Bentham 'Securities against misrule and other constitutional writings for Tripoli and Greece (ed. P.H. Scofield) part of The collected Works of Jeremy Bentham, 1990, Oxford, p193

pivotal to the proposed new constitution; Alexandros Mavrokordatos and Theodoros Negris. Despite his best efforts, however, Leicester was not an effective communicator and his arrogant manner was not conducive to good relations. Perhaps even a hindrance.

After he purchased an unattached Lieutenant Colonelcy, he served in Greece and his residence there appears to be of some considerable time, as reported in The Times on 5th July 1824:

"The Hon. Leicester Stanhope is arrived in town from Greece. We are happy to state, that whilst he makes no concealment of the difficulties with which the Greeks have to contend, he considers it impossible for the Turks to meet with success in the present campaign. Mr Stanhope's opinion on this point is of much value as he has long resided in Greece, and has taken a prominent part both in the civil and military department of the Government".[1]

Leicester may have fought alongside Lord Byron who was in Greece at this time. They had certainly met by November 1823 when both were at Cegalonia (Ionian Islands). Indeed, Leicester accompanied Byron's dead body back to England.

Stanhope was involved with an 8-year old Turkish boy,

---

[1]   Globe and Traveller. Cited in The Times, 5th July 1824

Mustapha Ali, who had been so traumatised by seeing his family massacred by the Greeks that he crept into the oven in the kitchen to escape the slaughter and by this means survived. He stayed in the oven for two days, fearful to stir and, when he did find the courage to emerge, Lord Byron heard of his plight and took the boy into his care.

Mustapha was with Byron at the time of his death and Stanhope took over care of the boy by bringing him back to England and urging his brother, 4th Earl of Harrington, to render assistance. The Duke of Leinster and his wife Hon Charlotte Augusta Stanhope, sister to Harrington and Leicester Stanhope, adopted the boy as a protégé and he was seated in the first coach after the hearse carrying Byron to his grave.[1]

Typographical Colonel

Other stories emerged about Leicester's time in Greece through 1823 and 1824. How he established a press and newspaper at Missolonghi.

His approach to Greece, however, fundamentally differed from both Byron and the Leader of the Western Greeks, Mavrocordato. His efforts to unify the west and east Greek leaders (Odysseus, Eastern Greeks) was not successful and his arrogance and condescension may

---

[1]   Lord Byron's Grecian Orphan, The Times, 15th July 1824

have aggravated parties, rather than helped.

Stanhope, as he had done in India, gave high precedence to promoting education of the Greek people. Byron gave him the nickname Typographical Colonel because of his promotion of Greek newspapers. The difference between them was that Byron thought newspapers could aggravate a fledgling constitution - as papers were foreign owned. Byron thought it was better to give priority to securing the military first and, in the end, Byron was probably right. Stanhope, with Bentham's help, persevered with his view on how Greek should develop and drew up a draft Constitution and presented it to their representatives.

In 1823 Stanhope (sensing that things were not going his way) wrote to Bentham saying "the spirit of monarchy or rather aristocracy seems to predominate Greece and I think the governments of Europe will endeavour to put one of their legitimates on the throne of this country. It must be our care forthwith therefore to engraft on the public mind those principles which contribute to the greater good of the greatest many".[1]

In mid 1824 the political climate disintegrated into civil war. Byron had been right and Stanhope's attempt to form a constitution was premature. His draft

---

[1]   Letters of Stanhope to Bentham, 1st December 1823 in Bentham Correspondence.

Constitution was not accepted amidst multiple difficulties. Loans to Greece were a stumbling block and, following the death of Byron, Stanhope was recalled to England, which he did with Byron.

Back in London, the Greek Committee wrote to Stanhope on 17th July 1824 thanking him for his "unwearied zeal, sound discretion and extensive benevolence ... whilst acting as Agent in Greece".

In October of 1824 he published a volume 'Greece 1823 and 1824' which comprised of a variety of letters and documents concerning the Greek Revolution.

On 6th July 1825 Stanhope attended the Royal Grand Gala Ball at St James's Palace along with 4-500 other guests and dignitaries. Leicester was residing, at this time, at Stable Yard, St James - the location of the first 'Harrington House'. The family would move their London residence to Craig's Court in the time of the 7th Earl.

Later that same year Leicester was appointed to a committee which had been tasked with raising a monument, by means of public subscription, to Byron. To commemorate the 'genius poet'.

In 1828 Stanhope was in Paris where he arrived with

Sir Francis Burdett of Foremark/Repton, an MP. His visit was described by the Countess of Blessington who told of Stanhope receiving much attention from the Duc d'Orléans.   The Countess said "Stanhope gave an account of Byron's death ….. the fine temper and good breeding that seem to be characteristic of the Stanhope family have not degenerated in this branch of it, and his manner as well as his voice and accent remind me very forcibly of my deal old friend, his father, who is one of the most amiable, as well as agreeable men I ever knew".

On 23rd April 1831 Leicester married Elizabeth William Green, only daughter and heiress of William Green and Ann Rose both of Trelawney, Jamaica.[1]

With his army career over, Leicester began a business venture in 1838 when he became a Director of the St. Marylebone Joint Stock Banking Company. In 1841, however, the company ran into financial difficulties and the shareholders filed a bill in 1842 against the directors "for the purpose of fixing certain losses on the directors personally".[2] Stanhope had wished to retire and wind up the company but the financial implications deferred the winding up process and several law suits dragged to

---

[1]   A Genealogical and Heraldic History of the commoners of Great Britain, vol 4 by John Burke of the Green family of Welbyr, Northants
[2]   Deeks v Stanhope, 14 Sim, 57

1851.[1]

In 1851 a case was brought, Clarke v Earl of Harrington regarding the sale of his brother Lincoln's riverside mansion, Putney House, one of the most prestigious houses in Putney. Lincoln had owned it since 1829 and it was frequently visited by King George II during hunts. There was some confusion as to whether an estate agent had secured the sale and was therefore entitled to a fee, but it was judged there was no evidence and so the court found in Stanhope's favour.

A few years later, Leicester and Elizabeth took up residence in a leased house in Chelsea:

Ashburnham House

Leicester, Elizabeth and their family were living at the very modern looking Ashburnam House in Chelsea from 1841 which they leased. The house sat in 11 acres of surrounding land and was by the King's Road.

---

[1]   Law Times, the Journal and Record of the Law and Lawyers, Vol. 17, dated 19th July 1851, p219

Finally in 1851, on the death of his brother Charles, the 67 year old Leicester came into his inheritance and became 5th Earl of Harrington and acquired the Stanhope estate at Elvaston Castle. A few months later, on 29th November, the new Earl and Countess held a feast in the gothic hall at the castle where 70 of their tenants were invited to dine and toast the Queen. The church choir sang the national anthem and Harrington declared his tenant farmers *"as religious, moral, industrious and as ancient a race of tenant-farmers as any that could be found in England"*. He told those gathered that he intended to build a school-house and said *"as we are all free men we must exercise their rights of voting at elections, unbiased by him. If, indeed, they asked his advice, he was accessible to all ... provided they would promise not to follow it if it did not coincide with their judgment."* He closed by saying he would visit all their houses and farms *"and become acquainted with them"*.[1]

His brother's magnificent 'secret garden' which had been secluded for so long was thrown open to public gaze as Leicester decided to open the gardens for the public to see, for an admittance fee of 3 shillings. Thousands flocked to see it.

---

[1]   Derby Mercury, 12th November 1851

Clockhouse

The Countess of Harrington meanwhile was busy with charitable concerns. She had a large house built about 1852 on the south-east perimeter of the Elvaston estate in Derbyshire, facing Main Road, specifically to provide accommodation for old retainers who had been employed at the castle. Known as the Clockhouse (as there is a large clock-face set in stone at the front) and, until recent times, had a stone inscription denoting the Countess's gift of the property. It is in close proximity to the school which was constructed about the same time.[1]

---

[1]   The Clock House, Elvaston. Grade II Listed Building since 1985. 7 Castle Court, Elvaston, Derby

Elvaston School

On the death of their son, Algernon Russell Stanhope, the Earl and Countess had a monument erected to him which is in St Bartholomew's Church.

Algernon died age 9 years in 1847. It is located in the chancel as a reclining figure, by Westmacott.[1]

It is said that Algernon's last words were "Lord Jesus receive my spirit".

---

[1]   Derbyshire History, Gazetteer and Directory, 1857

Algernon Russell Gayleard Stanhope, Viscount Petersham 1838-1847
Chest tomb by Westmacott, marble effigy

On acquiring the Elvaston estate, Leicester threw open the magnificent gardens to the paying public. A newspaper advertisement in the Leicester Journal for 6th May 1853 said:

"The Gardens at Elvaston Castle

> By the kind permission of the Earl of Harrington these gardens will be again Open to the public on Whit Monday May 16th, the entire proceeds to be appropriated to the fund for the erection of a parsonage house at Bosley, a small chapelry in the parish of Prestbury, near Macclesfield, Cheshire. Tickets of admission 1s each, may be had from Mr Barrow Elvaston; the booksellers, Derby

and near the entrance to the gardens. A Special Train will leave the Leicester Railway Station at 10am and Loughborough 10.30 am and return to Leicester at 5.30 pm. In addition to the attractions of the gardens, two bands will be in attendance and refreshments will be provided under the management of a committee."

Vicar v Countess

All did not go perfectly well, however, for the new Earl and his Countess.

In 1857 a wonderful, but satirical, description of Elvaston appeared in the newspapers describing this 'model village' with its Lord and Lady living at the castle, its vicar and curate ministering to contented parishioners, a village school supported by those from the great house, a subscription to restore the church, the vicar dropping in for tea with the Lord and Lady:

"O gentle Arcadia! O happy sheep and happy shepherds! Happy Elvaston! Happy is its Lord and Lady, whose title is Harrington - happy in its vicar-shepherd, whose name is Highmore - happy in its curate the shepherd lad, whose name is Jones ....."[1]

Of course, this scene of overflowing happiness is a romantic idyll, but it was also utter nonsense.

---

[1] The Saturday Review of Politics, Literature, Science and Art, Vol. 4 by John Douglas Cook, Philip Harwood, Walter Herries Pollock, Frank Harris and Harold Hodge

Considering the close proximity of St Bartholomew's Church, being just a few yards away from Elvaston Castle, there occurred in 1857 an extraordinary dispute between the Vicar[1] and the Countess of Harrington. The vicar seems to have been at odds with a large section of his parishioners and rumours abounded slurring the vicar's good name. It was said he had 'undue familiarity with a female servant' and stole the sacrament money. These rumours were repeated in a conversation between the Countess of Harrington and Mr Jones, the vicar's curate, abridged as follows:

"That man Highmore is so wicked, I never take the sacrament of him - he is so wicked. He keeps the sacrament money, and never gives any to the poor - he pockets the money given for church repairs. He is a drunken character - always playing at cards from morning to night, and gambling, and encouraging the people in drunkenness and debauchery. He and his wife are constantly roling drunken on the floor. He keeps a most disreputable house - is a mountebank and a rider at Astley's".[2] The Countess further associated the vicar

---

[1]   Frederick Nathaniel Highmore 1804-74: Sherborne, MA 1838 second Master Wimborne Grammar School, Ordained Deacon 1837, Priest 1838, Head Master of the Royal Grammar School in Burnley, Lancs. 1839-41 Vicar of Elvaston, 1841-73 Senior Chaplain to the Earl of Harrington, died 27th December 1873 at Thurlestone Grange, Derby. Alumni Cantabrigiensis, Vol. 2. Married 25th April 1843 at Elvaston to Margaret Anne Robinson

[2]   The Saturday Review of Politics, Literature, Science and Art, Vol. 4

with a lady called Ellen Winson. Astley's was a circus, so Lady Harrington was saying the vicar was akin to one of the characters who rode bare-back on horses in the circus arena.

Jones claimed that on 12th April 1857, in a meeting with Lady Harrington when she was thus describing Highmore, that he told her *"how wicked it was to circulate such slanderous and false reports".*[1]

Jones was affronted by the slander, on two counts. He felt the allegations reflected badly on the vicar who he considered a man of the highest standing but also, as his curate, that he too was tainted by the rumour of theft. Lady Harrington told Jones the curate that the reason she refused to attend church and take the sacrament at the vicar's hands was because of his immoral character.

Jones the curate was disturbed by what he had heard and, in a conversation with the vicar, he revealed Lady Harrington's comments. The result was that Rev. Highmore brought a legal action of slander in the Court of Common Pleas against the Earl and Countess of Harrington.[2] The case of Highmore v Harrington took place at Derby Assizes and, since it boiled down to the

---

[1]   The Standard, Wednesday September 9, 1857
[2]   Cases Argued and Decided in the Court of Common Pleas in the Michaelmas Term, 1857, Vol. 91

word of the Countess against that of the Curate, then Mr Jones' testimony was pivotal.

All attempts by Jones to assuage the Earl by explaining his difficult position failed. He wrote long letters, printed in the 'Daily News', justifying himself and explaining the circumstances and addressed every detail but, in reply, he received curt, rude responses from the Earl. Reverend Jones explained how he could not ignore the allegations that had been made, because *"so many and such fearful and severe charges have been uttered by Lady H against the character of Mr Highmore"*.[1] He then went on to assure the Earl that he had personally spoken to Highmore who had satisfied him that all the sacrament money was properly accounted for.

Jones then spoke to the Countess to tell her she had been misinformed but she *"persisted in her opinion"*. As Jones wrote this first letter to the Earl, he had already heard that Rev Highmore was bringing legal action against the Harringtons and Jones was to be called to give evidence. Jones said to the earl "As a clergyman, however, my duty is to seek peace and ensure it and, if I can, at this eleventh hour, bear the olive branch in this case".

The Earl's response was short and haughty: *"I know*

---

[1]   First letter between Mr Jones and the Earl of Harrington, from the Daily News

nothing of Mr Highmore, except as our parish priest. You were received at my board as a friend. You listened to the discourse held, and you now tell me that you have divulged what you heard there, find it to be incorrect and hold out to me 'the olive branch'. Ask the first gentleman you meet what he thinks of my conduct and of yours".

Jones replied on 23rd June 1857 with another long explanation. In respect of Lady Harrington being 'misinformed', Jones cited the Bible *"if any brother trespass against thee, go and tell him his fault between thee and him alone"* to justify his telling her she was misrepresenting the vicar. Again, his lengthy explanation and appeal to be a peace-maker met with short shrift. Writing on the 24th June, Harrington said *"As to your peace offering - I have not declared war, and should be the last to sue for peace. Mr H lives in a glass house, and should not throw stones. I care nothing about your evidence. Before you apprised me of your hostile intentions I regarded you as a friend; I now look upon you as an enemy, but bear you no malice."* Palace Gardens, 24th June 1857.

Jones tried again and wrote a third, long letter in response to the Earl on 29th June and, the following day, received another short reply in which Harrington sarcastically asks *"What is your opinion about introducing two swindling parsons into a pulpit?"*

The fourth letter from Jones, dated 4th July introduced the subject of names entered on the rate book. Jones had taken over the property formerly tenanted by Jonathan Severn but which had, improperly he said, been entered under the name of the Earl of Harrington. Jones hinted that *"this has in the new rate book been altered, I hear by the authority of your lordship, which means you will pardon me for saying that an irregularity equivalent to an illegality, has been committed"*.

The Earl replied the following day and the thrust of the Harringtons' case was that the conversation between the Countess and the Curate was private, as the Earl told him: *"Your conversations with Lady H were private. You are now going to make them public, and as you hope, to make them appear libelous. You boast of doing so, but in the court you will blush. I pity you. P.S. you are silent about the two swindling curates."*

This was all getting too much for Jones who could see his explanations were fanning the fire and not putting it out. Writing on 16th July 1857 Jones said, *"My Lord, I feel great uneasiness in continuing this correspondence with your lordship .... No good can, I fear, result for the exchange of letters.... Your lordship has had every opportunity of criticizing the circumstances, and you have not hesitated to apply a severity of unjust accusation with regard to them…. And further, if it should so happen that I have to blush in court, it will be, my Lord, not for any act of my own, but for the woeful character of the statements that a lady of dignity and exalted position has condescended improperly to make".*

The case of slander proceeded to the Derby Assizes where it was found in the Vicar's favour and he was awarded damages of 750*l*. The Harringtons immediately launched an appeal on the grounds that the damages had been excessive, but they were denied a new trial. Justice Cockburn said *"if the jury believed that Mr Jones's evidence was true, I think it impossible that we can say the damages are excessive. My own impression is, that juries are hardly liberal enough in these cases".* The evidence provided by Jones was *"worthy of belief"* and *"that being so, I have no hesitation in saying that, looking at the destructive and fatal tendency of the imputations cast upon the plaintiff as a clergyman and a gentleman, the damages which the jury have awarded him are anything but excessive".* Another Judge concurred, Justice Crowder saying *"the charges being so serious, I entirely agree with my Lord in thinking that the damages are far from being excessive".* Goliath was slain.

The Saturday Review, in examining the conduct of the Countess in this matter compared the language used by the lady of Elvaston with that heard at Billingsgate *"both exhibit the redundancy and elasticity of the English language"*. That the Countess had expressed herself strongly, too strongly, and grossly exaggerated as a means 'merely' to make herself understood. She had, however, been taken literally by the good curate Jones and the Harringtons paid a hefty price for her indiscretion.

As for Highmore (giant-slaying David), who had been appointed by Charles, 4th Earl of Harrington, he continued as Senior Chaplain to the 5th, 6th and 7th Earls of Harrington until his death on 27th December 1874 at Thurlston Grange, though how the Earl and Countess got on with him after these events is hard to imagine.

Maine Law Man

It is tempting to think that Harrington disliked all parsons as he certainly had a terrible track record of challenging them. In January 1857 he was approached by the vicar of Ockbrook, Rev. Scott, who had asked him to contribute to the Borrowash National School. This school was necessary to accommodate the children brought into the village by parents (indeed children were employed too) seeking work in the Earl of Harrington's cotton factory in that village.[1] The vicar

---

[1] DRO D664M/T121-122, Earl of Harrington leased Borrowash Mills (water corn mill and lace thread mills) to John Harrison Towle of Draycott, lace thread

was probably fairly confident that his appeal would receive a warm welcome, but it did not. Instead, the Earl refused to help, saying that he could not *"subscribe to any clergyman who did not use his influence, in the pulpit or on the platform, to support the Maine Law and Band of Hope schools"*.

The good Reverend Scott was livid at Harrington's reply and told him bluntly that he believed it was his duty to assist the village since the very need for a school had been created by the Earl's own factory employees settling there. He went on *"but if your lordship really thinks that no education at all is better than an education not based on these new principles of total abstinence &c or that the clergy, who do not, unhappily, quite coincide with your lordship's view on that open question, are to be left to struggle on unaided with the burden of the national education on their shoulders, why then I have nothing more to say, though not because I can conceive such opinions to be reasonable"*. Scott went on to say that he would rather not receive any assistance from the Earl than take it at the price of his freedom of opinion.

Harrington, of course, could not let the matter settle there, he took the opportunity to reply and launch into

---

manufacturer and Henry Neville Towle of Wilne Mills, gent, lease for 10 years from 1861, 1872 an evangelical promotion of the Maine Law and the evils of drink. Only then, after offending the vicar and preaching to him about his beliefs, did he say *"If, notwithstanding, you can give me any sound reason for not adopting it* [the philosophy of Maine Law]*, I will immediately subscribe to your school."*

To his credit, Scott stayed focused on the topic and challenged Harrington's beliefs directly. He stated his objections to the Maine Law; *"I doubt its possibility, its principle, its fairness, its working and its necessity"*. Harrington responded by further extolling the virtues of temperance, telling the vicar that there were 380 public houses in Derby which might easily be converted to coffee houses. He said *"Nay, I contend that the clergy are indirectly supporting inebriety by not joining the enlightened religionists who advocate the cause with such wonderful success."*

By Scott's next letter, it seems clear from the tone of it that he sees he is 'flogging a dead horse'. He said *"it ill becomes those to quarrel who have, in fact, the same great cause at heart; and quarrel with your lordship I will not, however your lordship may endeavour to pinch and coerce me."* The surprising conclusion to this head-butting correspondence was, in fact, that Harrington did offer a subscription to the school, but failed to win over the Reverend Scott who stuck to his own principles and, if he ever was in receipt of funds from the Earl, Scott made not one jot of difference to his curriculum to accommodate Harrington's wishes.

In another incident, the Earl extolled the virtues of being teetotal but refuted that he was a Teetotal Peer. Writing in the Derby Mercury on 8th April 1857 the Earl responded to another writer only identified as 'Parson Pop' and he rebuked the writer for categorizing him as such, rather calling himself a Maine Law Man.

In 1858 the Earl was a speaker at a meeting of the United Kingdom 'Alliance' in Derby, a temperance movement seeking the prohibition of the trade in alcohol. He began his speech by saying *"Neighbours and Friends: All persons agree that the drinking habits of the people are the great first cause of most of the evils that afflict the country. We are therefore met here to promote temperance and the Maine-law as the best means of effecting that object, together with the Permissive Bill ..."*. He finished his speech by saying *"Gentlemen, we have all of us heard fervent patriots sing and declare that 'Britons never shall be slaves'. False. False! Says the demon alcohol, You are my veriest, my abject slaves. With my delicious epicurean poisons I captivate your souls; my lieutenants watch over my alcoholic fountains. They exercise a powerful influence in electing your Members of Parliament; and these wise gentlemen tax you by millions for these drinks. Huzza, then, for free-trade in alcohol ..."*

In his later years, in 1859, the 5th Earl purchased Washingley Hall in Huntingdonshire, a mansion he restored in 1861.

Washingley Hall, Huntingdonshire

He was not to enjoy it for long, however, as he died the following year when it was then passed on to his son Sidney, 6th Earl, and after that it went to the 7th Earl, Charles Wyndham, who sold it in 1870 to J C Dymoke Roberton. The house was demolished sometime in the 1950s.

Leicester was residing at the Harrington's town house in London in 1862 when he died on Sunday night 13th September. His body, however, was returned to Elvaston for burial in the family vault. His coffin was led by a procession of four priests and also William Barron who carried the coronet and cushion, Barron being the 4th Earl's favourite gardener. He was carried by six garden labourers but only a handful of relations were present, as the Earl had directed that his funeral be private.[1]

After his death, in 1881, census records show widowed Elizabeth residing at the family's London residence of Harrington House, Palace Gardens, along with her daughter Geraldine who had married Edward Nugent Leeson, 6th Earl of Milltown. Leeson was Lord Lieutenant of Wicklow, Knight of the Order of St Patrick and, later, an honorary Commissioner in Lunacy. The couple had no children and the Milltown title went to another relation before it expired.

Elizabeth, now the Dowager Countess of Harrington lived on until January 1899 and, after her death in London, her body too was transported to Elvaston for burial. The body had been put into a leaden coffin which enclosed an oak coffin with a breast plate stating "Elizabeth William, Countess of Harrington, died December 1898, 87 years". It arrived by special train from St Pancras to Derby Midland Railway Station and was conveyed from there to Elvaston by a transparent hearse. The coffin was taken directly to the church

---

[1]   Derbyshire Advertiser and Journal, 19th September 1862

where a few locals had gathered to see it interred in the family vault. The occasion was described as being a January day of semi-dark dreariness with few relations in attendance at a service. Her heavy coffin was placed directly over that of her late husband, 5th Earl. Over the vault, there is a marble tomb under a canopy representing John Stanhope who died 1610, and also a semi-recumbent effigy of Sir Michael Stanhope. Seymour Sidney, 6th Earl who is about to be discussed, would later have his remains buried there too.

Leicester, 5th Earl of Harrington

Monument to the earl's wife Elizabeth who died on 7th September 1898.

SEYMOUR SYDNEY HYDE STANHOPE, 1845-66,

6th Earl of Harrington

Seymour Sydney Hyde Stanhope was born on 27th September 1845 at Ashburnham House in Chelsea which was a property his father had leased from at least 1841. The family's occupation of Ashburnham may have been confined to the period 1841-47 because, after that, the death of the 4th Earl in 1851 meant a major upheaval for the family as they assumed the Elvaston estate. Seymour succeeded to his father's title and estates in 1862, long before he had reached his full age.

Seymour attended Christ Church, Oxford, after which time he went on a shoot to Scotland with his friend the Duke of Hamilton. Seymour seems to have contracted what was thought to be a cold whilst in Scotland. When back in London he consulted his doctor who advised him that respite in a warmer climate during the winter months may be beneficial. Consequently Seymour made his way to Cannes in the south of France but it quickly became apparent that he was not suffering from the common cold as his condition worsened rendering him weaker and weaker. He died in Cannes at just 20 years[1] of age, probably of consumption, on 22nd February 1866.

---

[1] The Gentleman's Magazine, Vol. 220, p583, dated 1866

His death without heirs and being unmarried sparked a chancery case on 15th April 1871 between the Countess of Harrington v Earl of Harrington: that is to say, Elizabeth Stanhope (mother of Sydney Seymour Stanhope) versus Charles Wyndham Stanhope (cousin who inherited the title and became, no doubt to his consternation, the 7th Earl of Harrington).[1] Elizabeth Stanhope was son Seymour's administrator and brought proceedings against Charles Wyndham over the furniture and chattels of her son claiming they were the property of the 6th Earl in descent from the 3rd. In the Will of the 3rd Lord, it was said "I give and bequeath to my said trustees .... in trust for the person and persons who for the time being shall under or by virtue of, or under, the limitations in any, settlement of my said mansion house at Elvaston, and the estates in the said county of Derby settled therewith, be in the actual possession of the same mansion house and estates, to the end and intent that all and singular such personal property may be deemed and considered as heir-looms, to go along and forever be used and enjoyed with the same mansion house and estates, so far as the rules of law or equity will permit, but so nevertheless as that the same chattels personal shall not, as to the effect or

---

[1]   The Weekly Notes: being Notes of Cases heard and determined by the House of Lords, The Superior Courts of Equity and Common Law, the Courts of Probate and Divorce, the Chief Judge in Bankruptcy and the Admiralty and Ecclesiastical Courts, Part I, 15th April 1871

purpose of transmission, vest absolutely in any person who, under and by virtue of any settlement, shall or may become seised of, or entitled to, the said mansion house and estates for an estate of inheritance, in possession or reversion or otherwise, unless such person shall attain the age of 21 years, or, dying under that age shall leave issue inheritable under the limitations in any settlement thereof."

In response to Elizabeth Stanhope's Bill, Wyndham filed a counter-claim for the same possessions stating they were his as part of his inheritance. The case seemed to rest on the fact that Seymour had died under full age but the Chancellor decreed in favour of Charles Wyndham. The Countess, though she appealed the decision, failed to change it.

Sydney Seymour had died seven months short of his 21st birthday and was therefore a minor. A memorial brass was erected to his memory at Elvaston Church, against the north chancel which contains an effigy depicting him in academic attire. [1]

---

[1]	Kelly's Directory of the Counties of Derby, Notts, Leicester and Rutland. Published London May 1891, pp203-4

Sydney Seymour Hyde Harrington

CHARLES WYNDHAM STANHOPE 1809-81,

7th Earl of Harrington

Charles Wyndham Stanhope was born in London in 1809 on 16th August, the eldest son of Rev. Hon. Fitzroy Henry Richard Stanhope (Dean of St Burian in Cornwall and Rector of Catton in Yorkshire) and Caroline Wyndham. It is apparent that, for most of his life, he never really expected to inherit the earldom and Harrington estates as he would have been expecting his cousin Seymour Stanhope to have lived a long and fruitful life. However a combination of Seymour's early death and the death of various uncles meant the title and estates descended to him when he was 57 years of age. The previously mentioned lawsuit by his cousin's mother suggests the sudden change in direction of the inheritance did not meet with universal approval within the family.

Charles attended Eton and Magdalene College Cambridge[1] and served as a Magistrate in Derby as well as Deputy-Lieutenant of Derby. He also met William Gladstone who recorded the fact on Monday 19th December 1831: "Breakfast with Martin who was very kind to me, rode with Wood & Wordsworth. Dined at the Lodge - evening at Wood's & supper - met the Greys,

---

[1]   Alumni Cantabrigienses, Vol. 2

Cavendish, Stanhope, Hallam &c"[1] - Stanhope was described as a conservative.

On 15th January 1839 Charles married Elizabeth Still de Pearsall (eldest daughter of Robert Lucas de Pearsall of Willsbridge and of Wartensee Castle, St Gall, Switzerland) at the British Consulate in Paris and the couple went on to have ten children. Most of the children were born in Ireland where the family resided from the period 1844 to 1862 at Strangford in County Down on the east coast of Northern Ireland. An entry in Alumni Cantabrigiensis for Charles states him to have been farming near Belfast in 1860.

He was described as being of "remarkably amiable disposition, fond of out-door exercise, especially of yachting and driving and taking much interest in the improvement of his estates and the welfare of his tenantry".[2] Charles was a keen yachtsman and on 25th July 1874 it was reported that he had taken possession of a new screw steam-yacht called 'Bessie' which was lying off Southampton. Whether his wife shared his fascination for sea-faring vessels is hard to say because whilst he was away enjoying his new yacht, the Countess and family were residing at Stanhope Lodge,[3] West

---

[1]   The Gladstone Diaries: 1825-32 by William E Gladstone, Oxford University Press. 15th February 1969

[2]   Derby Mercury, 29th June 1881

[3]   Formerly Grove House

Cowes, Isle of Wight where the family had another residence[1] and where they spent their latter years. Charles, 7th Earl's creative bent was for making and playing violins.

Harrington House, London

The town address for the Stanhope family had been Harrington House at Stable Yard, St James (next to Buckingham Palace), the same address his grandparents had stayed at before their despatch to Dover Castle barracks.

Former Harrington House, 3-4 Craig's Court, London[2]

---

[1] Illustrated London News, 25th July 1874
[2] Picture courtesy of Richard Jones, who went out of his way just to take this picture for us - with enormous thanks

However, it was Charles who moved residence for the Stanhopes a short distance away to a new property after 1868, again named Harrington House, but located at 3-4 Craig's Court in London. The freehold land had been bequeathed to the Stanhope family in the Will of General Francis Craig to 3rd Earl of Harrington though it was not until the 7th Earl's time that the family took possession.

In 1866, shortly after the young 6th Earl's premature death, Charles took over the title and estate and on 8th August of that year called a Court Baron at Sawley to meet his tenants. He was not personally in attendance, being away in London on parliamentary business, but others in attendance included a variety of solicitors and local gentry.

Harrington had appointed Mr Leech as his Steward and a large number of the manor's copyhold tenants were in attendance. 13 jurors were sworn in and reminded that it was their duty to inform him of the death of any tenant and telling them what business was expected of them. A dinner followed. Leech told those assembled that the Earl had come into possession of large estates and the copyholders of the manor would find "that a real Stanhope had succeeded to the title of Harrington", probably this was intended to be a distinction between the new 'mature' 7th Earl and the 6th

Earl who was a young man barely full age when he died. The Earl and his Steward wanted to encourage enfranchisement, whereby copyholders could become freeholders on payment of one and a half year's rent. Those present cheered the Earl but condoled over his recent loss of a favourite child.

Not long after he became earl, an invitation was extended to the children of the Shardlow Union Workhouse to attend the house and estate for a fun day out. The children were given a tour of the gardens followed by party games and food.[1]

The 7th Earl died at Harrington House on 26th June 1881 at the age of 71 years from congestion of the lungs.[2] A few weeks before that, he and his family had been present at their country residence in Elvaston, as indicated on the 1881 census taken on 8th April of that year. He had been attended for some weeks by the Derby Doctor W G Curgenven who looked after him at Elvaston Castle.

7th Earl of Harrington's Arms

---

[1] Derby Courier, August 1866
[2] Derby Mercury, 29th June 1881

The family lived in some style with 9 family members being attended by 29 staff, mostly under the age of 35: Butler, Under Butler, 2 Valets, 2 Footmen, Housekeeper Annie Ford, Cook Emma Daniels, 3 lady's maids, 4 house maids, Kitchen maid, scullery maid, dairy maid, 2 Still room maids, 4 laundry maids, steward's room boy, 2 porters and a governess.

Also in the family's service, but in other buildings nearby the main house, there were 8 grooms, a coachman & his wife, head gardener John Herbert Goodacre & family, 5 gardeners, farm servant indoor, gardener domestic, timekeeper & wife, watchman, farm servants, farmer, 8 agricultural labourers, head game keeper, game-keeper, keeper, cowman, joiners, dressmakers, brick layers, apprentices, blacksmith and wagoner.

The probate inventory at the death of Charles Wyndham, 7th Earl, shows him in possession of Elvaston Castle, Harrington House at Charing Cross, Gawsworth in Cheshire, Stanhope Lodge at Cowes and, of course, 'Bessie' the yacht.[1]

Elizabeth lived on for many years, dying eventually in February 1912 at West Cowes on the Isle of Wight.[2]

---

[1] TNA: D518M/F189 Probate Inventory of Charles 7th Earl of Harrington
[2] Cornishman, 8th February 1912

About 1880, size 7.5 x 5 inches
Published by William McKenzie, 69 Ludgate Hill, London
Plate, 'A Series of Picturesque Views of Seats of
Noblemen and Gentlemen of Great Britain and Ireland'
Edited by Rev. F.O. Morris

CHARLES AUGUSTUS STANHOPE, 1844-1917,

8th Earl of Harrington

Charles was born in 1844 in Clontarf, near Dublin, Ireland[1] and attended Queen's College, Belfast as well as Christ Church Oxford for part of his education. His father's unexpected inheritance of the Harrington earldom and estate necessitated the family's relocation to Elvaston Castle in Derbyshire after 1866. He was known to be a keen polo player, a sport he commenced whilst in Malta in 1875. He was part of teams that won the Gloucestershire County Cup in 1885 (playing at the back), Derbyshire County Cup, Hurlingham Champion Cup at Sussex and the Rugby Open Cup with Cheshire.

Polo games were arranged at his Elvaston estate on his 'perfect ground'. He was the President of the County Polo Association and the first President of the Polo Pony Society. He is attributed with inventing papier-mâché goal posts and established the Polo Pony Stud Book.[2] His presence on polo fields was described thus: "his rotund figure and flowing beard were a feature on British grounds".[3]

---

[1]   As stated by him on the 1911 census
[2]   Polo in Britain: A History by Horace A. Laffaye
[3]   The Polo Encyclopaedia, 2nd Ed. By Horace A. Laffaye

He was described in Baily's Magazine, *"In every matter connected with the horse, its breeding, breaking, and use, no name is, perhaps, better known, none more respected than that of Charles Augustus Stanhope, eighth Earl of Harrington".* He was also called *"a sportsman to the backbone, a thoroughbred gentleman, manly in bearing, kind, frank and courteous in manner, with a kind word for everyone and a harsh one for none, and generous to a fault"...* and *"one of the most popular men in the county, a universal favourite, and respected by everyone".*[1]

He married Eva Elizabeth Carrington youngest daughter of Robert, 2nd Lord Carrington on 12th July 1869 at the Strand in London but the couple had no children.

Although Elvaston Castle in Derbyshire was the seat for the Earls of Harrington, the family held more lands in Cheshire and had another seat at Gawsworth. Charles went into the army and by 1880, in the Boer War, became a Major and Hon. Lieut. Colonel of the Earl of Chester's Yeomanry Cavalry. In fact Charles had assisted in raising the 21st and 22nd companies of Imperial Yeomanry. It was said that Charles donated 'a sovereign for each trooper as pocket money'[2] and that he 'swept the board' at the Military Tournament.

---

[1]   Derbyshire Advertiser and Journal, 9th June 1893
[2]   A History of British Cavalry, Vol. 4: 1899-1913, p92, by Lord Anglesey

In 1881 he inherited the Harrington title and estate following his father's death and on 15th August 1881, made his first appearance at the House of Lords.[1]

On 29th December 1882 the Earl distributed a pound of prime beef to every working class member of Elvaston parish (some 320) and, on Christmas Day, the Countess gave sixpence and a bun to each of the 103 children attending Elvaston School.[2]

At his death, the 8th Earl's estate comprised of: Elvaston Castle in Derbyshire, Gawsworth Hall near Macclesfield in Cheshire and Harrington House at 4 Craig's Court in London.

8th Earl of Harrington, taken in 1884, from Baily's Monthly Magazine of Sports and Pastimes 'Earl of Harrington'

The family's estates comprised of 4,569 acres in Derbyshire, 8,138 acres in Cheshire, 196 acres in Durham, 38 acres in Northamptonshire and 3 acres in

---

1   Hansard, Records of the House of Lords, Vol. 264, c1878
2   Derbyshire Advertiser and Journal, 29th December 1882

Leicestershire.[1]

On 8 December 1881, the Hunting Appointments listed in the Derby Daily Telegraph listed the Meynell Hounds meeting at Elvaston Castle on Thursday 8th December and, on the resignation of Mastership of the South Notts Hounds, by Lancelot Rolleston, Harrington took over and held the position for twelve seasons where it was said he 'hunted the country generally five days a week'. Other reports say he hunted twice a week.

In 1898 on 12th January, Lord Harrington led a large group assembled for a hunt. Meeting at 11am in the Market Place at Newark, at the invitation of the Mayor who fêted them with drinks, the party set off for a hunt. The following year, 1899, a similar assembly of hunters gathered at Breadsall where Harrington was again Master. The list of those attending was a veritable who's who of notables of Derbyshire and environs and despite the hunt riding through an enormous area viz: Chaddesden Wood, Birch Wood, Spondon Waste, Dale Hills, Stanton, Hopwell, Risley, Breaston, Sawley Gorse and the osier beds between Sawley and Wilne (Harrington land), not one fox was found.

In 1907 a polo match took place between the House

---

[1]   DRO: GB026 D664M, Stanhope of Elvaston

of Commons and the House of Lords for the Earl of Harrington's Challenge Cup. The match took place at Ranelagh and was a clear victory for the Commons.

In the left picture is the House of Commons team with the unmistakable figure of a young Winston Churchill on the right. The right-hand picture is the House of Lords team with the Earl of Harrington being second from the left.[1]

Charles had wider interests than just sport; he wrote to the Morning Post in 1899 at the beginning of the Boer War urging more to be done for national defence by encouraging people to learn to shoot at ranges to augment the country's home defences. He also had an interest in engineering and invented a steam-powered lawn mower and was said to have invented a self-opening gate. It is thought he died from burns received

---

[1] The Graphic, July 13th, 1907

in one of his own amateur experiments.

After the death of Charles 8th Earl without children, his title and estate passed to his brother Dudley.

DUDLEY HENRY EDEN STANHOPE, 1859-1928

9th Earl of Harrington

Dudley Stanhope was born on 13th January 1859[1] in Ireland to Charles Wyndham Stanhope 7th Earl of Harrington and Elizabeth Still de Pearsall. He might not, like his father before him, have expected to inherit the Harrington earldom as his older brother Charles Augustus held the title and was married. Dudley was 60 years of age when his brother died childless in 1917.

On 26th April 1883 he married Kathleen Wood, daughter of Joseph Carter Wood of Felcourt, Sussex and they had three children.

Known as "Old Whiskers" due his prominent white beard, Dudley was a popular figure and skilful at woodcarving. Some of his work remains in Elvaston Church where he restored the carved chancel screen and the cross on it. He was also a very keen huntsman and ordered his dogs to give chase on the first suitable day after his funeral, which they duly did.

---

[1] Birth location taken from the 1901 census

The 9th Earl's younger brother Hon. Lincoln Edwin Stanhope 1849-1902 had joined the army by 1871. He married Helene de Bravura in 1885 and Lincoln died by accidental drowning.

He had a daughter Eva Barbara Edwina Stanhope 1890-1977 who was married at Elvaston Castle - perhaps one of the last family events to take place there:-

Bertram Marion Crawford 1890-1952

Son of Francis Marion Crawford 1854-1909 (American novelist, historian and linguist who lived in Italy) and Elizabeth Christophers Berdan (daughter of the American Civil War General Hiram Berdan.)

Eva Barbara Edwina Stanhope & Bertram Marion Crawford
Marriage at Elvaston Castle in September 1921[1]

---

[1]   The Tatler, September 1921

As a younger man, Dudley had been involved in a scandal. A young ballet dancer by the name of Charlotte Blackman "had been seduced by Dudley Stanhope, son of the Earl of Harrington".[1]

Later testimony said "the Hon. Dudley Stanhope had been the dupe of that woman (Miss Blackman) who, while she was acting at a provincial theatre, had got him behind the scenes".[2] Charlotte had given birth to a child around 1880-81 and Dudley arranged, through his solicitor George Lewis, for the child to be supported in 1881 with a deed giving the mother £150 by three instalments. Blackman, who relocated to Liverpool, needed an advance on her instalment and asked the National Advance Bank of the Strand for a loan for £15, using the deed as security. Subsequently, however, she defaulted on repayment and a much larger sum was demanded in settlement. A writ was issued against poor Charlotte and a judgment was found against her.

Dudley's son Talbot Fitzroy Eden Stanhope, of the 2nd Rifle Brigade, was killed in action on 9th May 1915 at Ypres. His name is commemorated at the Belgian memorial at Ploegsteert (8 miles from Ypres). He was an Old Oakhamian, having attended Oakham School in

---

[1]   Boardroom Scandal: The Criminalization of Company Fraud in Nineteenth-Century Britain by James Taylor, 2013
[2]   The Law Journal, Vol. 18, p212

Rutland and was just 18 years old when killed in action.

Five years after inheriting the title and estate, Dudley sold a painting at Christie's, called 'Portrait of a Man', oil on wood for £399 to Frank T Sabin of London. The provenance shows the portrait descending from Leicester Fitzgerald Stanhope 5th Earl to Dudley and the sale particulars state that the portrait was believed to be of Protector Somerset.[1]

The Earl died at Elvaston Castle after a long illness on 14th November 1928.[2]

---

[1]   Image available via the Metropolitan Museum of Art www.mtmuseum.org
[2]   Western Daily Press, Bristol, 14th November 1928

CHARLES JOSEPH LEICESTER STANHOPE, 1887-1952, 10th Earl of Harrington

Charles Joseph Leicester Stanhope was born on 9th October 1887 at Westminster, at the Harrington family's home there. A few years later, on the 1891 census, he was resident with his family at Watchfield House in Farringdon, North Bedfordshire being waited on by five servants. Ten years later, still just 14 years of age he was living at Bartley Close, Copythorn in the New Forest at Southampton, now attended to by six servants.

He became Captain of the 15th Hussars, Reserve of Officers and was awarded the Military Cross. He also served as Deputy Lieutenant of Derbyshire. The 1911 census shows him in military barracks at London on 2nd April of that year, rank 2nd Lieutenant in the 15th Hussars.

On 23rd April 1919 he married Margaret Trelawney at Holy Trinity Church in Upper Chelsea and, at the time of marriage, he gave his address as 141 Sloane Street and his mother Countess Harrington signed the marriage register as a witness. Margaret's address at marriage was Bulyard and her father was Major Henry Herbert Douglas Seaton who married in September 1895 at a double wedding in Bournemouth (his wife was Ethel

Rosaline Leigh-Hunt) and the other couple at the wedding were Beryl Leigh-Hunt and Cyril George Dedgson of the Indian Civil Service. Both brides were dressed alike in white duchess satin with long trains and white feathers with orange blossom.

A son born to Charles and Margaret died a few days after being born but the following year there was another son born, William Henry - the future 11th Earl of Harrington.

Charles was strapped for cash and so when a proposition was put to him by Sir Julien Cahn, to borrow and rent some of his collection of oil paintings, the proposal was readily accepted. Twenty world-renowned paintings were sent to Cahn including: 'Tangier' by Sir Peter Lavery; 'The Children of Charles I' by Sir Anthony Van Dyck (1634); self-portrait by Peter Paul Rubens (1628) and portrait of the Duchess of Cleveland by Sir Godfrey Kneller (1705). Eleven portraits: Queen Henrietta Maria (wife of Charles I) by Sir Anthony Van Dyck (1633); portrait of Charles II by Sir Joshua Reynolds; portrait of the Duke of Grafton by Sir Joshua Reynolds; portrait of a lady in a ruff holding a glove by Hendrik van der Vlient (1625) and a portrait of Lady Stanhope called 'Contemplation' by Sir Joshua Reynolds. The 'renting' of these portraits continued after the Earl's unexpectedly earth death through to the tenure of the young 11th Earl and the arrangement only ceased when Cahn himself died in 1944.[1]

In 1928 his father, 9th Earl of Harrington died, and Charles inherited the title and the estate and soon after took his place in the House of Lords for the first time. There is no record of him actually speaking in the Lords. He was not, however, destined to hold the title Earl for long and he died aged just 42 years, when he broke his neck in a hunting accident. It was reported on 24th October 1928 that the Earl was lying seriously ill at Elvaston Castle and showed no sign of improvement, so he may have lingered a considerable time after the accident before he died.[2]

His funeral was attended by many hunts. The coffin was preceded by the kennel huntsman and whip in scarlet.[3]

Wife Margaret lived on for many years and remarried to Luke Lillingston (who hunted with the Irish Meath hounds in the 1930s). Margaret died on 15th September 1952.

---

[1] The Eccentric Entrepreneur: Sir Julien Cahn: Businessman, Philanthropist, Magician and Cricket-Lover, 2008 by Miranda Rijks
[2] Nottingham Evening Post, 24th October 1928
[3] Western Daily Press, Bristol. 20th November 1929

WILLIAM HENRY LEICESTER STANHOPE, 1922-2009
11th Earl of Harrington

Bill Stanhope was born on 24th August 1922 and, by the age of 7, had lost both his father and grandfather. He succeeded to the title as 11th Earl of Harrington and inherited the family's estates - though perhaps it is more pertinent to mention that the loss of his grandfather and father within one year brought the insurmountable problem of double death duties to the family at a time when the young earl was still a minor. It really is a miracle that Elvaston Castle has survived at all because so many of England's stately homes succumbed to the clutches of developers and urban sprawl or faced decay and demolition.

'The Boy Earl' - 11th Earl of Harrington acting as a Steward
at the Harrington Hunt Point-to-Point at Aston.
Seen on the right leading the field of the first race to the starting gate[1]

---

[1]   Derby Daily Telegraph, 22nd April 1931

After attending Eton and Sandhurst, he joined the police force, as he was too young to join the army. He served as Captain in the 15th/19th Hussars and was deployed in the Netherlands, Denmark and Germany and later saw service in Palestine. He served as no. 2 to Major Rathdonnell of Lisnvagh in County Carlow.

He married Eileen Foley-Grey on 5th February 1942 at Westminster and the couple had three children (two girls and Charles Henry Leicester who would become 12th Earl of Harrington). The Earl was granted a divorce decree in 1946 on the grounds of adultery by the Countess with John Bissill, a professional jockey who was named as co-respondent and who did not defend the petition.[1] He was granted custody of the couple's three children and awarded costs.

After divorce in 1946, Bill married on 24th January 1947 to Anne Theodore Chute at Westminster and had three more children (again two girls and a boy). Divorce in 1962 was followed by his third marriage on 14th October 1964 to Priscilla Margaret Cubitt at Kensington (two more children).

Hansard records for the House of Lords make reference to Lord Harrington on 27th October 1955 in the course of a debate on a proposal to establish a

---

[1]   Nottingham Evening Post, 19th November 1946

guided missile range in the Hebrides. There was concern about the impact such a scheme would have on the crofters there and there had been hostility to the proposal from locals and Harrington had spoken out at concerns.   The missile range's purpose would be to enable operational training for troops and in a speech by Lord Carrington, he said "There is no suggestion that missiles are going to be exploded on St Kilda, as the noble Earl, Lord Harrington, thought. We expect to have about twenty men there during the summer months, taking care of a radar station".[1]

Bill has been actively involved in equestrian matters for many years and raised funds in the 1960s to enable Ireland to take part in a 3-day International Event Team at an Olympic Games and he organised the first 3-day International Event at Punchestown in Ireland. He had his own commercial stud in Limerick (Greenmount) and was Chairman of the Bloodstock Breeders' Association. From 1972-93 he was Master of the County Limerick Foxhounds and was involved in the formation of the Clonshire Equestrian Centre (through the County Limerick Hunt Club). He served again as Master of the County Limerick Foxhounds from 1997-2001.

In 1967 he inherited additional titles of 8th Viscount

---

[1]   Hansard, Report of Debates in the House of Lords, 27th October 1955, Vol. 194, cc75-108 line 104

Stanhope of Mahon and 8th Baron Stanhope of Elvaston when his cousin James 7th Earl Stanhope died.

He died on 12th April 2009 at his home in Ballingarry, County Limerick, where he had lived since the 1930s, and his funeral was at Adare where well over 1,000 people were in attendance.

The present 12th Earl of Harrington is Charles Henry Leicester Stanhope.

LEGACY

The marriage of the 3rd Earl of Harrington to Jane Fleming brought assets to the Stanhopes which, even today, are the bedrock of their fortune. 52 acres of land in Kensington was purchased by Sir John Fleming in 1754 and he expanded his holdings in 1763 by purchasing the adjoining 23 acres (in the area today of Queen's Gate). Sir John died shortly afterwards and his daughters acquired a section each. Jane Fleming, of course, married Charles 3rd Earl of Harrington and that is how the Stanhopes acquired their portion; her sister Seymour Dorothy Fleming married a Swiss gentleman and her portion descended to his daughter from another marriage.

In 1851 the 4th Earl and John Lewis Fleming divided what was known as the Harrington Villars estate which was then held in fee simple. The area can be identified by the retention of family names: such as Stanhope Gardens, Stanhope Mews, Harrington Gardens, Harrington Road, Harrington Court, Elvaston Place, Elvaston Mews, Petersham Mews, Petersham Place and

Petersham Lane. As the 4th Earl died that year, it was then passed on to the 5th Earl who commissioned builders to develop his 46 acres. Commissioners for the Great Exhibition of 1851 bought up all of the Villars estate and some 17 acres of Harrington's 46. Twenty-five acres of this prime land in South Kensington is still owned by the family today.[1]

---

[1]   www.british-history.ac.uk/survey-london/vol38/pp3-8

APPENDICES

ELVASTON NAMES:

Alewoldestune, Elwadeston(e), Erwardeston, Ailwaston, Aylwaston, Aylwaldeston, Aielwaston, Aylewaston, Ailwardeston, Aylwoldeston, Aylwarston, Eylwaston, Aylwaston, Eylwaston, Aylweston, Aylwayston, Elwaston, Elvaston (1493), Elueston (1577), Elverston (1641).[1]

ELVASTON FIELD NAMES:

Historic

Ansedeleg, ate Brugge de Thurlestone, Atterrathorne Field, Barley Flatt, Bradmere, Brademere, Broadarse Flatt, Brooke Pingle, Brugge de Thurlestone, Bryge Mylnes, Buls Close, Chalke Flatt and Way, Cole Flatt Furlonge, Coxon Close, Crabtree Furlonge, Domcliffe Closse, Dovecoate Close, Gall Furlonge, Greave Butts Furlonge, Hall Sich, Holes Closse, Kirkfield, Leech Poole, Little Shorte Leyes, Meane Mousehold Meadowe, Milnefield, Musewelle, Northolme Furlong, Ravenhow Stones, Sciterisflat, Sitchpoole Close, South End Lane, Stockland Hurst Furlonge, Syddich, The Challenge Gosse Furlong, the Long Holme Furlonge, the Round Closse, the Roundeaboute Closse, the Weare Arse Close, Wassell Butts

---

[1]   Keith Cameron's The Place-Names of Derbyshire. Part 2 (EPNS 28), Cambridge 1959 and TNA: E31/2/2/3445 folio 276v Domesday Book Entry

ELVASTON FIELD NAMES:

Modern

Blend Common, Bowling Leys, Breach Field, Butcher Lane, Butt Lane, Carr Close, Causeway, Chickin Holme, Church Leys, Emmett Nooks, Flax Leys, Foofin Close, Fowlhurst Knowl, Foxley Hursts, Goty Field, Greavy Hole, Greenway Closes, Hill Closes, Horse Bridge, Kirk Ash Field, Larkin Close, Ley Closes, Madge Flatts, Meer Common, Middle Sicks, Moor Closes, Nether Fields, New Close, Rowley Cross Field, Sevenlands Close, Sheepcroft Common, Smithy Furlong, Swimsty Greave, the Ends, the High Meadows, the Hooke, the Inhams, the Juliams, the Nine Ridges, the Pingle, Thickrush Common, Tweenhill Closes, Winmill Moor Pingle.[1]

Stanhope burials at St Bartholomew's, Elvaston

STANHOPE

Anthony Ch27.
Alexander (Patron) Ch2; Algernon Russell Gayleard Ch7, Ch16, Ch25; Anne de Shelford Ch2, Ch9; Augustus Ch4; Carolina (Lady) Ch4; Catherine Ch9; Charles (Patron) Ch2, Ch8; Cordall Ch9; Cordella Ch9; Dorothis Ch9; Dudley (the Hon) Ch18; Dudley Henry Eden (the Hon) Ch24; Elizabeth Ch9; Fitzroy Ch4; Fitzroy Henry Richard Ch26; Francis Ch4, Ch9; Lady Geraldine Evelyn Ch25; Henry Ch4; Henry William Ch26; Jane Ch9; Johannes Ch8; Sir John (Patron) Ch2, Ch9, Ch27; Katarine Ch9; Kathleen Emily Ch24; Leicester Ch4; Leicester Fitzgerald Charles, G.B., K.C.S. (Col. the Hon) (afterwards 5th Earl of Harrington) Ch16, Ch25; Lincoln Ch4; Margreat Ch9; Michael Ch9; Olivia Ch8; Phillip (Sir) Ch9; Talbot Fitzroy Eden Ch20, Ch24; Thomas (Patron) Ch2, Ch9; Tos. HVMVS Ch9; Willi Ch9.

---

[1]   Historical Gazetteer of England's Place Names